HOME COM

The role of Red Cross Auxiliary Hospitals in the
North Riding of Yorkshire
1914-1919

Eileen Brereton and Anne Wall

"There is about the hospital as a whole a thing that is
typical of all these Red Cross Hospitals - an air of comfort,
supplementary to the actual provision of necessities"

'The Way of the Red Cross' published 1915

Published by   Eileen Brereton and Anne Wall in 2014
                      Second Edition printed in 2015

Copyright   © 2014-2015 Eileen Brereton and Anne Wall

ISBN Number   978-0-9931034-0-7

Layout and Printing by   Imprint Services
                          2, Anchorage Lane
                          Northallerton
                          North Yorkshire
                          DL7 8DX

Cover design by Phil Ogden with picture of soldiers in County Hall, Northallerton on front cover and on the back cover images from Ursula Lascelles' archive held at North Yorkshire County Council Record Office.

Every attempt has been made by the publishers to secure appropriate permissions for materials reproduced in this book. If there has been any oversight we will be happy to rectify the situation and a written submission should be made to the publishers at the email address below.

Orders and correspondence about this book may be sent to:
info@northridingvadhospitals.co.uk

Foreword

As we commemorate the outbreak of WWI, "Home Comforts" reminds us of the great efforts of people in the North Riding in setting up the important 'Voluntary Aid Detachment' auxiliary hospitals.

The authors/compilers have done a valuable job in piecing together stories of those who tended the men in their care. Perhaps this book will also encourage others to share their family memories and stories to create an ever more detailed record of this history.

My home, Crathorne Hall, was offered to the British Red Cross by my grandparents Lionel and Violet Dugdale. My grandmother was clearly a very 'hands on' commandant and was supported by other members of her family. She was awarded an OBE for her work at Crathorne. Her son, Tom, fought as a young officer at the Front for the last fifteen months of the war during which time she wrote to him every day. With life expectancy at the Front numbered in weeks she never knew whether each letter would be the last he would ever receive. He was one of the lucky ones who survived the war uninjured.

It is inspiring to read of the tremendous amount of voluntary work undertaken by the communities of the North Riding providing food, comforts and entertainment for the soldiers as well as fundraising for the relief of the injured. "Home Comforts" shows what a debt of gratitude we owe to those whose work on the 'home front' did so much to repair the damage, both physical and mental, of 'our boys at the Front' when they returned home as wounded soldiers.

James Crathorne,

Lord Crathorne KCVO
Patron of the North Yorkshire Branch of the British Red Cross

This book is dedicated to the young women and men of the
North Riding who gave their time freely to care
for the sick and wounded in W.W.1.

Contents

Introduction

The focus of our project was the discovery of the original First World War Report Book of the North Riding Branch of the British Red Cross. This gave details of the thirty two hospitals which had been created to care for the convalescent soldiers. There were not only the names of the auxiliary hospitals, as they were known, but also the members of the men's and women's Voluntary Aid Detachments (VADs) who served in them, as well as detailed local and county accounts.

As commemorative events are taking place throughout the country to mark the centenary of the outbreak of WW1, we decided we would investigate more of the history of the work undertaken by VADs in the North Riding. This would involve us visiting places across the old County area, such as schools, village halls, private homes, hotels and County Hall.

The many people we have met have generously shared photos, information and stories from their family histories. Local history groups and individuals have contributed pieces of the story, and we have been able to add to their findings about their own areas of research. We have been helped in many ways in this project by the North Yorkshire County Council Record Office, not least by them introducing us to the papers of Miss Ursula Lascelles who had been a VAD nurse at Swinton Grange. Her story proved to be an inspiration to us.

The Museum and Archives Department of the British Red Cross provided the details of the formation of the Voluntary Aid Detachments. They also found an album from Wydale Hospital, which is held there, together with the records of the nurses and VADs who worked in the hospitals, and details of the honours awarded to them.

As a result of this activity we felt we needed to put into print our research, so that people could appreciate the story of the devoted service which was so freely given towards the war effort in the North Riding.

Most of the buildings which served as auxiliary hospitals are still standing and we hope to increase the awareness of the important role they played by telling their part in this history.

The award of a Heritage Lottery Fund grant has enabled us to achieve the printing of this book, and supported the production of the materials that will enable us to share the story when we give talks and hold exhibitions in the local community.

As Red Cross Volunteers ourselves we have always had a sense of pride in belonging to a humanitarian organisation that helps people in crisis whoever and wherever they may be. Our admiration for the selfless activities of our Red Cross VAD predecessors during the First World War has highlighted the need for such service to continue long into the future, whatever that may hold.

RED CROSS AND THE ORDER OF ST JOHN OF JERUSALEM AUXILIARY CONVALESCENT HOSPITALS IN THE NORTH RIDING OF YORKSHIRE 1914-1919

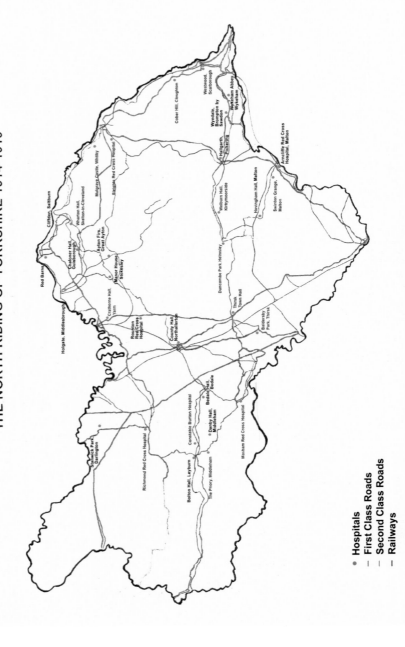

- • Hospitals
- — First Class Roads
- — Second Class Roads
- — Railways

The British Red Cross and the Function of the Voluntary Aid Detachments.

At a meeting on July 17th 1905 Queen Alexandra issued an appeal to all women in the Empire to take part in Red Cross work which she said "is essentially women's work and is the one and only way in which we can assist our brave and gallant Army and Navy to perform their arduous duties in this time of War."

In 1906 local branches of the British Red Cross were formed throughout the country following an appeal by the wives of the Lords Lieutenant of each County. In the North Riding this task was undertaken by Lady Florence Bell from East Rounton. She was to play a very important role as President of the North Riding Branch, as well as being the Commandant of the Red Cross Auxiliary Hospital at East Rounton for the duration of the First World War.

Voluntary Aid Detachments (VADs) were formed in 1909 as a joint initiative by the British Red Cross and the order of St John of Jerusalem as requested by the War Office. Initially this was to support the Territorial Medical Service in the event of a war but it became apparent that they could also play an important part in peace time too.

Detachments were formed that would fulfil the need for transport, nursing duties, equipment and contacts for troops. They were made up of separate men's and women's divisions, registered and numbered by the War Office. The men's divisions had odd numbers and the women's divisions had even numbers. The nursing section of these Detachments were also called VADs but were given other familiar names such as "very adorable darlings" or "the starched brigade"!

There were some famous names amongst the VADs such as Agatha Christie, Vera Brittain and Enid Bagnold. In fact, as Agatha Christie worked within the pharmacy setting, it was thought that this is where she learnt the properties of poisons that was to prove useful when writing her crime novels!

Composition of Detachments (1910 regulations)

Men	1 Commandant
	1 Medical Officer
	1 Quartermaster
	1 Pharmacist
	4 Section Leaders
	48 Men (4 sections of 12 men each)
TOTAL	56 Men

Women	1 Commandant
	1 Quartermaster
	1 Trained Nurse as Lady Superintendent
	(a certified nurse who has completed 3 years training at a hospital with a training school)
	20 Women of whom 4 should have cook qualifications
TOTAL	23 Women

The detachments were inspected annually and formed part of the technical reserve. Training courses and competitions were held to maintain proficiencies.

Training

Men were taught first aid by lectures and practical demonstrations. They were also instructed in transport and orderly duties.

Equipment required by the men's detachments included bandages, splints, rifles, swords, scabbards, bayonet (also used for improvising splints), carpenters tools, light ambulances, stretchers on wheels, ropes, poles and rings for improvisation, bell tents, hospital marquees and water tanks.

Women were taught first aid, home nursing, hygiene and cookery. They also learnt how to run a ward and many had some training within hospital settings. The War Illustrated Journal of 1914 stated that "since Florence Nightingale went with her knowledge, tenderness and high courage to tend our wounded soldiers at the Crimea, the part that women play in war has continued to increase in importance" and "both on the field and in the general hospital every woman used to deal with street accidents will be serviceable to her country as the soldier in the firing line".

Equipment required by women's detachments included bandages of all descriptions (loose woven, calico, unbleached, ordinary roller, special "T", many tailed) tourniquets, Indian rubber tubing, 2 dressing basins, first field dressings, materials to construct wooden splints and canvas for making sand bags.

In the minutes of the Red Cross Norton Division on August 14th 1914 it was recorded that all equipment was to be provided as far as possible by local efforts and in the event of difficulties the fact had to be reported to the County Director.

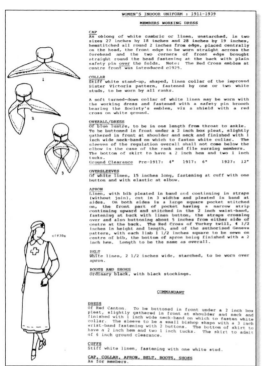

WOMEN'S INDOOR UNIFORM : 1911-1939

MEMBERS WORKING DRESS

CAP
An oblong of white cambric or linen, unstarched, in two sizes 27 inches by 18 inches and 28 inches by 19 inches, hemstitched all round 2 inches from edge, placed centrally on the head, the front edge to be worn straight across the forehead and the two corners of front edge brought straight round the head fastening at the back with plain safety pin over the folds. Note: The Red Cross emblem at centre front was introduced c1925.

COLLAR
Stiff white stand-up, shaped, linen collar of the improved Sister Victoria pattern, fastened by one or two white studs, to be worn by all ranks.

A soft turned-down collar of white linen may be worn with the working dress and fastened with a safety pin brooch bearing the Society's emblem, viz a shield with a red cross on white ground.

OVERALL/DRESS
Of blue lustre, to be in one length from throat to ankle. To be buttoned in front under a 2 inch box pleat, slightly gathered in front at shoulder and neck and finished with 1 inch wide neck-band on which to fasten white collar. The sleeves of the regulation overall shall not come below the elbow in the case of the rank and file nursing members. The bottom of skirt to have a 2 inch hem and two 1 inch tucks.
Ground Clearance Pre-1917: 4"   1917: 6"   1927: 12"

OVERSLEEVES
Of white linen, 15 inches long, fastening at cuff with one button and with elastic at elbow.

APRON
Linen, with bib pleated in band and continuing in straps (without join), cut in 3 widths and pleated in band at sides. On both sides is a large square pocket stitched on, the front part of pocket having a narrow strip continuing upward and stitched in the 2 inch waist-band, fastening at back with linen button, the straps crossing over and also buttoning about 5 inches from either side of centre at the back. The Red Cross of Turkey twill, 4 1/2 inches in height and length, and of the authorised Geneva pattern, with each limb 1 1/2 inches square to be sewn on centre of bib, the bottom of apron being finished with a 2 inch hem. Length to be the same as overall.

BELT
White linen, 2 1/2 inches wide, starched, to be worn over apron.

BOOTS AND SHOES
Ordinary black, with black stockings.

COMMANDANT

DRESS
Of Red Canton. To be buttoned in front under a 2 inch box pleat, slightly gathered in front at shoulder and neck and finished with 1 inch wide neck-band on which to fasten white collar. The sleeve to be a small bishop shape with a 3 inch wrist-band fastening with 2 buttons. The bottom of skirt to have a 2 inch hem and two 1 inch tucks. The skirt to admit of 6 inch ground clearance.

CUFFS
Stiff white linen, fastening with one white stud.

CAP, COLLAR, APRON, BELT, BOOTS, SHOES
As for members.

Uniform

This was provided for all personnel. The head dress worn by nurses changed, as the war continued, from short "dora" style caps to a longer veil that covered all of the hair.

The Red Cross emblem on the apron had to be sewn on separately. Younger nurses who wanted to appear more experienced often bleached their red cross so that it took on the appearance of a paler cross due to repeated washes!

At the beginning of the war the dresses were long but, as a shortage of materials developed, these then became a little shorter.

VAD Detachments

From the beginning of the 1st World War detachments were in such a state of readiness that they could immediately function in a very purposeful manner. This was not confined to just personnel but also to the provision of houses, halls, schools and other buildings that could be drafted in to fulfil the need for convalescent hospitals to cater for the wounded troops. These needed to be near a railway line for speedy access. It was seen as a necessary part of the war effort at home to offer these buildings for such a purpose. Many owners of stately houses in particular volunteered their houses and the "Lady" of the house often became the Commandant, wearing a very distinctive red dress as part of her uniform. These ladies, accustomed as they were to running large households, were ideally suited to arranging and running the hospitals and did so with great pride.

Apart from a Commandant the hospitals also had a medical officer attached to them, very often a local general practitioner, a matron and trained professional nurses.

BRITISH RED CROSS
WOMEN'S INDOOR UNIFORM: 1911–1939

MEMBER   COMMANDANT

Pre-1915
'Sister Dora'
cap

3

Initially there were some difficulties between the trained nurses and the VAD nurses due to the former thinking the latter were inexperienced empty-headed young girls!

Olive Dent in her article "Glimpses of VAD work" wrote that "VADs were of many social classes. They included women and indeed girls of title, women who were known and valued for their public service, professional women who abandoned work of lesser for that of greater importance, university graduates as well as stay-at-home girls who had spent most of their energies on sports."

Records at Devonshire House showed that many spoke fluent French, German, and sometimes Italian. They held certificates from the Institute of Hygiene, advanced physiology, first class cookery and housewifery diplomas, full massage diplomas and a few held degrees particularly useful for VAD work. It was thought good for young girls to experience the work in preparation for a future career. Olive Dent said that "the idea of a girl going to nurse at the age of eighteen is a trifle revolutionary but many long cherished notions have been set aside since August 1914."

In her book "A Nurse at the Front" Edith Appleton wrote that she considered "the VADs a source of great interest to me". She divided them into four sorts: "stallers", "crawlers", "irresponsible butterflyers" and the "sturdy Pushers".

However as the war progressed with large numbers of casualties and the increased experience of the VADs, the relationship between professional nurses and VADs improved on both sides. There is no doubt that, whatever the relationship between the staff of the hospitals, the wounded convalescing soldiers thoroughly appreciated the care they received from both groups.

The military authorities however were at pains to insist that the men should not be spoilt by the nurses as it might make them unmanageable and undisciplined and not fit to re-enter the harsh surroundings of the ongoing war.

Each hospital had a quartermaster who was responsible for the provision of supplies. In the Red Cross journal of 1st July 1917 (vol 4 no7 page 90) the responsibilities of the quartermaster were:-
    1, The catering.
    2, The issue of all groceries and stores, wines, spirits, and cleaning materials.
    3, The linen and clothing, soiled and clean, and their issue and repair.
    4, The equipment and its repair and upkeep.
    5, The pack store and the patients' kits.
    6, The destructor (incinerator)

The quartermaster also had to keep the books and produce a monthly statement of expenses. The two necessary attributes for the quartermaster to acquire according to this article were "a hard heart and a reputation for meanness in giving out stores."

4

It is reassuring to read however that they did not "turn an altogether deaf ear to the piteous appeal". There is an amusing description of items that accidentally found their way into the destructor!

QUARTERMASTER

(I'M THANKFUL ARE'NT YOU

SUCH A PERSON EXISTS

BECAUSE "QUACCA" WON'T DO)

The men's detachments provided support to the hospitals in many ways, though their numbers fluctuated due to enlistment and the need for men to be employed in their occupations as the war progressed. They were often the first people to meet the wounded soldiers at the stations and transport them to hospitals. This could be in motor vehicles, but in some cases involved a horse and cart. They also provided orderly duties in the hospitals and were particularly useful at night when they might keep watch over the wards, thus freeing up the nurses.

Both male and female detachments continued with training and were heavily involved in fundraising to support the work in the hospitals. They often marched in military parades to publicise their activities and collect money to continue their work.

Money was an important issue in the running of these detachments and the hospitals. The War Office provided three guineas a day for the care of the soldiers in hospitals but not all the hospitals took up this offer. Some of them provided care at the expense of the family who owned the house, which was much appreciated by the British Red Cross.

Other fundraising efforts took place such as "Our Days" where stalls and collecting tins, hog roasts, dancing, and other local activities were organised. Many of the communities provided food, clothing, medical supplies, equipment and soldiers' comforts using the money raised.

Work supply departments were set up in the country, which co-ordinated the production of essential supplies. These might involve making night clothing for the wounded soldiers or providing bedding.

Work parties also produced sandbags following guidance laid down by the authorities and woe betide the person who did not adhere to the pattern who could be made to feel that they had "let their soldiers down!" Collection of sphagnum moss took place in some areas, often by local schoolchildren. The moss was known to be a very useful wound dressing once it was cleaned and compressed.

BRITISH RED CROSS SOCIETY.

1914 (handwritten)

NORTH RIDING OF YORKSHIRE BRANCH.
H. M. LIEUTENANT :
SIR HUGH BELL, BT.

President :
LADY BELL.
ROUNTON GRANGE, NORTHALLERTON.

County Director :
MAJOR RUCK-KEENE.

Hon. Secretary :
MISS RUTHERFORD, GUISBROUGH.

June, 1915.

VICE-PRESIDENTS :

REV. THE MARQUESS OF NORMANBY
THE MARCHIONESS OF NORMANBY
THE MARCHIONESS OF ZETLAND
THE COUNTESS PERCY
THE LADY MARY FITZWILLIAM
THE VISCOUNTESS HELMSLEY *the Countess of Jarvik* (handwritten)
THE LADY JULIA WOMBWELL
THE LORD BOLTON
THE LORD DE L'ISLE AND DUDLEY

THE LADY DE L'ISLE AND DUDLEY
LADY EGERTON
LADY PAYNE-GALLWEY
LADY PEASE
MRS. CHALONER
COLONEL GODMAN, C.B.
MRS. JOHNSON
MRS. WHARTON
LT.-COL. WHARTON, V.D.

DISTRICT REPRESENTATIVES :

THE LADY MARY FITZWILLIAM
THE HON. MRS. CLIVE BEHRENS
LADY BERESFORD-PEIRSE
LADY WALKER
MRS. BELL-IRVING
MAJOR BOWER, C.M.G.
MRS. BOWER
MRS. BRENNAND
MRS. CHALONER
H. C. FAIRFAX-CHOLMELEY, ESQ. } (ACTING)
MRS. H. C. FAIRFAX-CHOLMELEY }
MRS. DUGDALE
MRS. FULLER
GENERAL HAMMOND
MRS. HEDLEY
MRS. WALTER L. JOHNSON
MRS. J. L. KIRK

COLONEL LODGE
MRS. WALTER LONG
MRS. CLAUD PEASE
MISS EVELYN PEASE
G. A. ROPER, ESQ.
MRS. ALBERT RUTSON
PENN C. SHERBROOKE, ESQ. *Dead* (handwritten)
MRS. STANCLIFFE
MISS AVERIL STOBART
MISS STOBART
LT.-COL. TATHAM
MISS AUGUSTA TINDALL
MAJOR-GENERAL SIR JAMES TROTTER, K.C.B.
MRS. TURNOR
MRS. WHARTON
MISS WILSON
MRS. D'ARCY WYVILL

Mrs Yeoman (handwritten)

The North Riding Branch of the British Red Cross was formed in 1907. In the Annual Report for the WW1 period the list of members of the executive includes families still in existence today.

Auxiliary Hospitals in the North Riding.

Initially there were twenty seven detachments in the Branch, eight mens' and nineteen womens'. The North Riding was a large county which then included Middlesbrough, the North East Coast, the Yorkshire Dales and Moors It was well served by a vast railway network. Near to these railway lines were numerous places that were offered as auxiliary hospitals.

These hospitals were catering for the ranks as officers were sent to several different establishments. The patients usually came from York, Leeds, and Newcastle military hospitals and were basically requiring convalescence and ongoing care in the auxiliary hospitals. At the beginning of the war many of the patients were Belgians and some of the Dales hospitals cared for those men and then closed down. They earned praise and thanks from the Belgian government for their efforts.

The first hospital to open was Swinton Grange, near Malton in 1914 and the last to close was Welburn Hall near Kirbymoorside in 1920.

By the end of the War, thirty two hospitals had been operating in the North Riding with 1,454 beds and the total number of patients cared for was 18,442 men. There is no doubt that the hospitals and staff were all appreciated by the wounded and sick soldiers who stayed in them. Some of these men had probably never experienced life in the country or lived in such grand houses but they always had a good word for the staff as seen in letters, gifts and the comments that they left in visitors' books or nurses' autograph albums.

Autograph Albums

Archives round the world contain examples of autograph albums in which officers and soldiers recorded their gratitude and affection to "their" nurses. The autograph album was important in a society that valued written messages of all kinds.

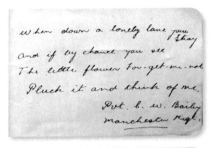

Visitor (at private hospital). "CAN I SEE LIEUTENANT BARKER, PLEASE?"
Matron. "WE DO NOT ALLOW ORDINARY VISITING. MAY I ASK IF YOU'RE A RELATIVE?"
Visitor (boldly). "OH, YES! I'M HIS SISTER."
Matron. "DEAR ME! I'M VERY GLAD TO MEET YOU. I'M HIS MOTHER."

Cartoons

Patient cartoons were a remarkable feature of the cultural and medical history of the First World War.

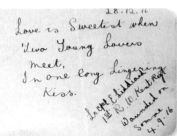

8

Redder, crosser Ladies.

Reddest, crossest Ladies

Red, Cross Lady

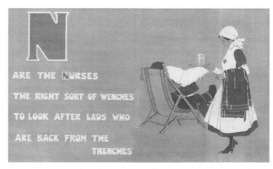

N ARE THE NURSES
THE RIGHT SORT OF WENCHES
TO LOOK AFTER LADS WHO
ARE BACK FROM THE
TRENCHES

"The Patient is not yet out of Danger."

"THEY'VE EVIDENTLY SEEN ME."

Tommy (dictating letter to be sent to his wife). "THE NURSES HERE ARE A VERY PLAIN LOT——"
Nurse. "OH, COME! I SAY! THAT'S NOT VERY POLITE TO US."
Tommy. "NEVER MIND, NURSE, PUT IT DOWN. IT'LL PLEASE HER!"

9

After the War many VAD nurses found it difficult to adjust to normal life again as the experience had opened their eyes to another life. Some solved this by enrolling to continue with nurse training and become professional nurses. Others missed the camaraderie and the feeling of usefulness that they had enjoyed even in the traumatic situations that they had found themselves in.

The North Riding Branch of the British Red Cross as a whole benefited from all the diligent work during the War and continued to run the detachments providing training and using the experience gained to further their caring work.

Food for Recovery

The value of feeding the convalescent soldier nourishing, easily digested food had been learnt from Florence Nightingale in her 'Notes on Nursing'. In 'War Illustrated Journal' it was stated that "strong intelligent girls who have gone through a good cooking class could soon be shaped into very helpful nurses at the battlefields. Our injured worn out troops often require delicate feeding more than the services of a trained hospital nurse. Their fagged out bodies could not for the time digest the ordinary rations. Yet if their strength is to be quickly recovered they must be at once fed on fresh well cooked food."

VADs were encouraged to complete a course in invalid cookery, following the British Red Cross cookery manual. Pride was taken in the quantity and quality of the food provided, especially in the hospitals which were in rural areas where perhaps local produce was more plentiful.

The kitchen at Welburn Hall

M. Oxford in her lessons for VADs wrote "it has to be impressed on everyone who takes up nursing that food for an invalid must be perfect of its kind and served up

10

daintily. Taste it before you take it to your patient, so that you may be sure the beef tea has enough salt in it and that the milk is not the least bit burned."

JUGGED HARE.

Cut the hare into pieces, but do not wash it; a small onion; thyme; parsley (shred very fine); pepper and salt (as much as will lie upon a shilling); ½ a nutmeg (grated); and some lemon peel (grated); a little fat bacon, cut in thin slices.

Cover it altogether close, and put the jug into a pot of cold water. Set it to stew gently for 3 hours, then put in ¼ lb. butter and shake it well several times. Send it to table served in a deep dish. Make forcemeat to serve with it.

L. H. L.

Milk was believed to be easily assimilated and therefore suitable as a diet for a great variety of cases. As well as incorporating milk into many recipes such as milk posset, junket, and arrowroot cup, each man was also encouraged to drink three pints of milk a day. The necessity of this was, however questioned in an article published by the British Medical Journal, but for those with serious mouth and jaw injuries feeding with milk two hourly provided some nourishment. The job of feeding the soldiers was usually given to the VADs who were seen as "mothers" and "comforters", but were supervised by the trained staff, seen as having more knowledge about nutrition.

In view of the many generous gifts of food, which have been sent to the patients, we think it would interest many people to see the following specimen of a week's Menu.

SPECIMEN WEEK'S MENU.

SUNDAY	Breakfast.	Sausages.
	Dinner.	Hot Beef and Kidney Pie, Plum Pudding
	Supper	Cold Beef and Pickles.
MONDAY	Breakfast.	Cold Ham.
	Dinner.	Liver and Onions, Treacle Pudding.
	Supper	Sausages.
TUESDAY	Breakfast.	Eggs.
	Dinner.	Hot Roast Beef, Yorkshire Pudding, Fruit Tart.
	Supper	Mutton Pies.
WEDNESDAY	Breakfast	Eggs
	Dinner.	Boiled Mutton, Sponge Pudding
	Supper	Hash or Cold Mutton.
THURSDAY	Breakfast.	Ham.
	Dinner.	Hot Roast Beef, Milk Pudding
	Supper	Cold Beef.
FRIDAY	Breakfast.	Eggs.
	Dinner.	Fish, Boiled Cod, &c. Jam Roly Pudding
	Supper	Soused Herrings.
SATURDAY	Breakfast.	Bacon.
	Dinner.	Hot Roast Beef, Treacle Pudding.
	Supper	Soup.

Duncombe Park 1916

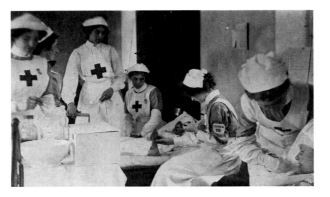

To make food more digestible, recipes using agents such as Bengers, malt extract and liquor pancreaticus were included. Peptonisation was a process where one glass tube of peptonising powder was added to each pint of milk, gruel, soup or beef tea.

Sugar was a greatly prized commodity. Puddings and jam sandwiches were welcome and necessary fare for the men. Plum jam in particular was plentiful and popular. Quantities of sugar for fruit preserving were obtained in Middlesbrough in 1917 through the Food Production Department of the Board of Agriculture. In 1918 the scheme was extended to distribute preserving sugar to fruit growers, and in the following year the general public were allowed a quantity dependent on the number in the household and the amount of fruit to be preserved.

In the summer of 1916 the Royal Commission for the supply of sugar was established as the forerunner of rationing. Sugar was in short supply everywhere and the hospitals were asked to supply statistics of the beds occupied and the number of staff so that each hospital could receive a fixed rate per head. The sugar was received monthly or quarterly from the nominated sugar brokers in London, Liverpool, or Glasgow.

BRITISH ✛ SOCIETY.

HOVINGHAM HALL HOSPITAL.

The Committee acknowledge, with thanks, your kind gifts

of _plums, cigarettes & 2 pots of jam_

Sept 25

However, as the sinking of merchant vessels became more frequent, supplies in the country became more inadequate and by the spring of 1917 the system was failing. After urgent and persistent appeals to the recently appointed Food Controller, Lord Rhondda, an arrangement was put into place for the hospitals to receive their supplies via a newly created branch of the Ministry of Food, a scheme which worked well to the end of the war.

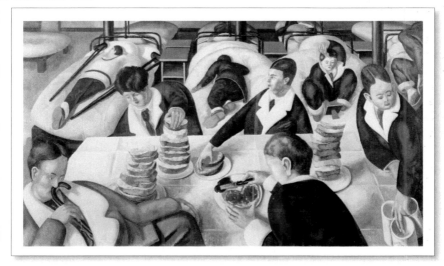

by Stanley Spencer

13

Many auxiliary hospitals received generous donations of food stamps from the local population to supplement their ration. In the "Malton Messenger" in January 1917 thanks were recorded to individuals and villages for food sent to Hovingham hospital every week including bread, cake and pastries, eggs and rabbits, vegetables and sweets.

Eggs were used liberally in hospital recipes. Coddled eggs featured, as did "nourishing Fillip for 4" which required 4 whole eggs and 3 lemons to be left, covered in a bowl for 3 days, being turned daily. When the shells had dissolved the mixture was beaten well, and strained into a jug. 2 saccharine tablets, half a pint of brandy and one pint and a half of milk were then added to the fillip mixture, bottled and administered in doses of one glass, twice a day.

During April 1915 a movement began for a constant supply of fresh eggs for the convalescent soldiers in hospitals throughout the country. 200,000 eggs were needed each week. These were delivered to local elementary schools and then collected for distribution.

During the first five months of 1916 the children of Raydaleside near Bainbridge sent 1,198 eggs to be collected, and from March to May the children of Askrigg had sent 449.

In December 1917, Sir F. Colchester – Wemyss K.B.E. was appointed by the Central Joint VAD committee as the Director of Food Economy at the Auxiliary Hospitals. A system of control was inaugurated, requiring monthly rates of consumption in each hospital to be submitted by the Commandant. This arrangement halted waste, prevented extravagance and also checked the rare occurrences of low consumption. A standard level of "adequate diet" was being provided in the majority of hospitals, based chiefly on the calorific values of the food served. It was drawn to the attention of the hospitals that they were allowed 8ozs. sugar and 8ozs meat (including bacon) per patient per day, but otherwise there was no real rationing. Later, however, the War Office did issue a minimum

"PLEASE MA, CAN'T I HAVE A LITTLE BROTHER?"

"WHAT? WITH EGGS AT 3D. EACH! NO, CERTAINLY NOT!"

and maximum dietary scale for all hospitals, including those for Officers. As food shortages increased, the Ministry of Food guaranteed the release of foods which were otherwise difficult or impossible to procure.

With apparent relief Sir F. Colchester – Wemyess, after admitting some trepidation at taking on such a potentially unpopular task, and anticipating resentment from the hospital Quartermasters and Commandants at the imposition of tedious paperwork and restriction, was able to report "from the beginning to the end I have experienced hardly anything but kindness and support." He was also thanked, having handled such a mass of monthly figures and obtaining 99% returns.

By 1917 the price for the general public for bacon, ham, lard, cheese, margarine and butter was fixed by the Ministry of Food. "Control Tea" was almost unobtainable, being offered in Middlesbrough at 5 shillings per pound until the price was fixed at 4 shillings. Bread cost 9d for a 4lb loaf, relatively lower than most other foods, which resulted in demand outstripping the supply of flour. As a result, in 1918 it was permitted to use potatoes in bread making to bulk up the mix, producing a dark, rough texture and unpleasant flavour, but by June supplies were improving.

In the North Riding, Captain and Mrs J.G.E Gardner were responsible for the distribution of sugar until the end of the war. This was a time consuming task for which they earned special thanks from the County Director of Red Cross Major R.L. Bower in his final report of 1920.

In the North Riding Auxiliary Hospitals during 1918 the bacon, cheese, sugar, dried fruits and methylated spirits for cooking were distributed from the County Director's office.

Messrs. N Russell and Sons, Northallerton and in particular Mr. L.W. Atley, Quartermaster of the Yorks./ 21 Voluntary Aid Detachment, were thanked for the efficiency with which bacon and cheese were distributed, and Mr. Fairburn was thanked for supplying the methylated spirits.

Comforts for the Troops

Throughout the war women and children "did their bit" for the war effort by knitting and sewing garments for the troops both at the Front and in the hospitals at home. They made sandbags, collected food for convalescent soldiers, raised funds to buy equipment and comforts for the use of the soldiers, and collected sphagnum moss to be used as wound dressings.

The first organised voluntary works in Middlesbrough, possibly even in the North Riding, was the War knitting group in the Winter Gardens. Initiated by Lady Bell, with Mrs Calvert as co-president, 146 ladies met on Tuesday afternoons from October 1915. Socks and helmets, gloves, mufflers and operation socks were knitted, and vermin shirts and Serbian blankets sewn.

Materials were paid for by public subscription until government wool from the Municipal Authorities became available. Originally everything was sent to Northallerton where Miss Atkinson had set up the Voluntary Workers Association, until a Middlesbrough Branch opened in 1915.

The Mayoress of Middlesbrough Mrs W.J. Bruce, set up "Middlesbrough hospital and clothing fund" for servicemen in hospitals.

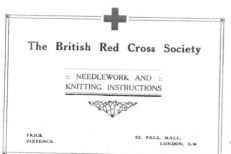

Teachers and scholars in the elementary schools were volunteers producing almost 18,000 items by the end of the year.

Meanwhile, throughout the North Riding, Red Cross working parties raised the money to pay for 2,500 garments – pyjamas, helpless case day and night shirts, vests, pants, ward slippers, day and bed socks, cushions, crutch pillows, arm slings and bandages were all sent to the Headquarters of the British Red Cross in London for distribution to the Front.

Queen Mary's Needlework Guild Middlesbrough Branch opened in September 1916 and by the time it was disbanded in January 1919 had sent 62,754 articles including bandages, swabs, pneumonia jackets, plugs, shell dressings, stretcher quilts, cushions and dressing gowns to the Surgical Requisites Association Head Depot in Chelsea to be distributed. Members of the Guild could buy a handsome enamel badge depicting a red and white rose, the crown, and a pin with the Guild's initials.

By the end of the war the British Red Cross had sent a quarter of a million knitting pamphlets, and twenty four million military garments were received.

Hints for Needle-workers - *The Times September 9, 1914*
EC, 3 Palace Green writes - 'Hundreds of socks for soldiers are passing through my hands, and may I ask all those who are so generous in these gifts, if they would kindly sew each pair together at the foot and at the top of the leg, and not to pin them together with pins, wire, darning needles stuck through cards with the remainder of the wool for darning socks? Hands and arms of receivers are covered in scratches in taking out all the pins'.

Whilst Doctor A. F. Wright of Welburn, York writes 'those who are making jackets for the wounded not to make them from red material, as red is extremely irritating to the central nervous system'.

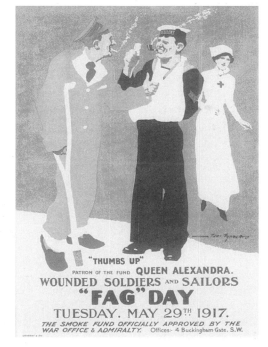

May 29th 1917 was officially nominated as "Fag Day" to raise contributions for the smoke fund which was officially approved by the War Office and the Admiralty, with Queen Alexandra as patron.

As reported in *The Times*, 'Smokes for Soldiers and Sailors "SSS" based in London raised funds to distribute 8 million cigarettes, 14,200 lbs of tobacco, 20,000 cigars and 1,160 dozen pipes free to over 700 field dressing stations, hospitals and convalescent homes at home and abroad, and hospital trains and ships'. By the end of the war more then a billion cigarettes had been distributed.

In Brotton during May to November 1915, monthly parcels of comforts were sent to the Front paid for by public subscription averaging £10 per month. Oxo, and Swiss milk was sent to France as well as the knitted balaclavas, mittens, socks and helmets.

Recognising the need for fresh fruit and vegetables for the fleet, Lady Bell set up an enterprising collection of gifts of green vegetables. A depot was opened in Middlesbrough market place to receive vegetables. From there they were sent to the River Tees Naval Base, to be distributed on His Majesty's ships from 1915 to 1918. In the Malton area, Mrs Lascelles, with Gladys Wood went with Miss Alexander's donkey cart round the farms to collect any fruit and vegetables that could be spared, such as apples, rhubarb and turnips. Some 30 tonnes in all were packed by the ladies and sent to the depot which had been set up in Malton by the grocer Thomas Taylor. From there the sacks and boxes were sent by train to Immingham docks for any ships of the fleet which were in port at the time.

Christmas 1915 saw the Rev. A.S. Brooks and Mrs Lascelles of Slingsby donating 313 plum puddings to the men on the battleship, 'Indefatigable'. The puddings were made by Mrs Lobley and boiled in Mrs Lascelles wash house copper, and Mr W.M. Marshall drove the consignment to Malton. The ship was lost at the battle of Jutland the following year.

Sandbags
In April 1915 Miss M.L. Tyler of Highgate London, prompted by an appeal from the wife of an artillery officer requested sandbags to be produced. She asked for people to make them to be sent out to the Front "because the artillery are almost more in need of sandbags than the infantry for they have the huge guns to cover as well, and they are not "dug in" to the extent that the men in the trenches are."

An infantry Lieutenant also wrote, "We want a tremendous lot of sandbags. Our division alone has been using a million a month. If you saw a shell burst on a parapet with sandbags, and on one without, you would soon see how many lives they save."

However, the sandbags had to be made to exacting standards otherwise they did not fulfil their purpose of protecting the troops. Careful measurements were insisted upon, otherwise the bags had to be re-sewn or rejected. If the opening was any lower than 14" they could not be filled with earth by a spade, and if the bags were stitched with fine cotton instead of string or thread they would soon unravel. The quality of the hessian was vital as, if it was not made of 100% jute, it would not be strong enough to withstand bullets.

Towards the end of January 1917 the military authorities asked Middlesbrough schools to make sandbags. Schools acted as depots for distributing materials and collecting the bags for the railway company to transport. Material was supplied by the military, string was bought in town and the children bought the needles. The juniors sewed the bags at school in the evenings and on Saturdays. One boy, laid up with a poisoned foot, made 45 sandbags and 162 grenade bags.

The total number of bags dispatched to Malton on 24th May 1917 was 71,266, (an average of 4½ per school child over 7 years old) and 70,548 grenade bags. 16 tons of material had been handled and £120.11s.1d worth of string used.

Representatives of Middlesbrough school boys record the total of 12,242 sandbags and 8,129 grenade bags made by boys at Ayresome School, Archibold, Linthorpe St Philomena's and Crescent Road.

Transport.

Bringing the wounded and ill soldiers from the Front line to the Auxiliary Hospitals in the North Riding entailed long and painful journeys for the men, cared for by nurses, doctors and groups of volunteers including VADs.

Injured men first had their wounds dressed at the Regimental aid post which were almost on the Front line, in large shell holes, disused trenches or derelict buildings. Anti-tetanus injections and pain relief was given in the Advanced Dressing Stations which were set up further behind the lines in underground bunkers or disused buildings. As soon as possible the men were then sent to the Casualty Clearing Stations(CCS) by horse drawn ambulance, lorry or railway. The CCS were set up in schools, convents or factories and had operating theatres and fully trained staff. On the western front this transfer typically took between 8 and 12 hours.

When they were fit enough to be transported by train they were sent to base hospitals for treatment before being either returned to the fighting or sent home. Gallipoli soldiers might face a voyage by sea of 2-3 days before being admitted to hospital. There was an acute shortage of hospital trains early in the war, necessitating the use of ordinary carriages and even cattle trucks where the conditions for the wounded were altogether inadequate, with straw for bedding.

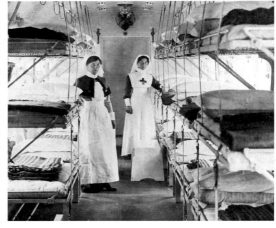

In 1915 the UK Flour and Millers Association presented the Red Cross with 2 especially built and equipped ambulance trains, which were sent to France. The War Office commissioned 30 standard ambulance trains, which had 16 cars, a pharmacy and 2 kitchens. 36 beds were arranged in 2 tiers in each ward, accommodating 400 injured men on each train, either sitting or on stretchers.

The Lancashire and Yorkshire Railways Companies ambulance trains were finished throughout with white enamel and had the luxury of portable fans. Ash trays were fixed next to each bed, and in photographs vases of flowers could be seen. However the conditions were overcrowded with men with wounds which had often not been re-dressed since their first treatment in the clearing stations, and many had chest infections and infected wounds. The stench of bleeding and festering wounds, very basic sanitary arrangements and cigarette smoke created a very different environment from the one projected to the public when invited to visit the new trains for the payment of sixpence.

The Friends Ambulance Units staffed many trains under the jurisdiction of the British Red Cross. The VADs and FAUs lived on the trains permanently tending their patients who had shrapnel and bullet wounds, gas injuries (which led to respiratory infection), frost bite and trench foot, with the complications of infections and gangrene. Some trains were equipped with a padded space for men suffering from shell shock. The staff had to endure broken nights, low temperatures and the constant difficulty of maintaining clean conditions with little water and many dirty, infected, infested men. Many of the men were desperate for water, due to dehydration which even necessitated locking water taps to conserve supplies.

The trains were fumigated with burning sulphur in an attempt to control the fleas and lice and each bed had a spittoon to receive the phlegm. The uniforms of soldiers who had been gassed presented a particular hazard to the nurses, as they could in turn be affected by the soaked uniform as they were cut off the men and the gas re-vaporised.

Having reached the ports, the trains were greeted on the stations by VADs and other volunteers serving hot drinks and handing out cigarettes to fortify the men for the next leg of their journey home. The men were transferred to the hospital ships, sailing across the channel. In the early part of the war the ships were painted gleaming white and green, with scores of brilliant green and red lamps slung along their length, including a prominent illuminated red cross.

"The deck of the British Hospital ship is one of the most cheerful places in the world. Every man is at rest after toil, is about to see friends after separation, can smoke when he likes, and has in every other man on board a companion with whom endless reminiscences can be exchanged and perhaps the merits and demerits of the Ypres salient, or the most adventurous use of tanks, warmly debated as is the custom of the Privates in the new army. Silent or vocal agreed beatitude fills the vessel."

However, as the war progressed hospital ships were torpedoed by the enemy, so their lighting was dimmed, walking wounded wore lifebelts at all times if their injuries permitted, and all stretcher cases had a belt under their pillow.

— A "BLIGHTY" —

In Blighty or Arriving on Home Shores.
Between February 1915 and February 1919 1,260,506 casualties were handled by railwaymen at Dover. 4,076 boats of injured men were unloaded and loaded onto 7,781 ambulance trains for the journey to the receiving stations on the East Coast main line.

Those men who needed hospital care were sent to military hospitals in York, Leeds or Newcastle. The soldiers were collected from the local railway stations by members of the men's detachments, using either motorised or horse-drawn ambulances. However the Pickering Detachment, which undertook the transport of convoys arriving for the Hallgarth Hospital, had no suitable wheeled vehicles so all stretcher cases had to be hand carried a considerable distance.

In response to the nationwide shortage of ambulances, on October 2nd 1914 an appeal, to which The Times Newspaper gave its powerful assistance, was issued by the British Red Cross to provide motor ambulances. In three weeks funds were raised to buy 512 ambulances with the Red Cross buying practically every suitable chassis in the country.

PRICE LIST.

"ASHFORD" LITTERS (*Continued*).

Fig. 49.—Wheeled litter.

A new and further improved pattern under-carriage has recently been introduced, having the two legs on each side coupled, so that when one is raised or lowered that on the same side at the other end of the under-carriage is also raised or lowered. This pattern is recommended with confidence, as the coupling is found to materially simplify the handling of a litter, owing to the fact that it gives to one man complete control of the four legs from either end. The mechanism is unavoidably somewhat more elaborate than in the ordinary pattern, but with reasonable care it is not likely to get out of order.

The extra cost is £1 10s. 0d. per litter.

Together with the Denis Bailey Fund launched in 1915 and the Transport of Wounded Fund, which included all The Times subscriptions earmarked for transport of the wounded, personal donations and £185,670 from the British Farmers' Fund, the total reached £1,159,941.10s.7d.

The expenses of equipping the ambulances included ambulance rings at 5/6 each stretchers £2.3s.6d, canvas for stretchers 19/- and dressings, bandages and tourniquets £4.0s.9d.

During 1918 the VAD men met 252 cases at Malton station, of whom 122 were transported to Swinton Grange Auxiliary Hospital, and 130 to Arncliffe Red Cross Hospital in Malton. In Saltburn and Skelton, members of the detachment were inspected in June 1918 by Major R.L. Bower, County Director, and Major General W.G.A. Bedford D.D.M.S where they had prepared four wheeled wagons and coup carts to transport all the wounded as well as equipment.

The motor ambulance of the Yorks/5 VADs in Redcar travelled over 1,600 miles in 1918, including conveying 21 wounded soldiers from Redcar station to Red Barns Auxiliary hospital in Redcar.

In Northallerton, 750 hours of escort duties were provided in 1918 alone, distributing men to auxiliary hospitals both inside and outside the North Riding. 29 convoys, in all about 300 men, were transported to County Hall or the Rutson Hospital (which was not administered by the Red Cross).

From January 3rd to November 25th 1918 in Thirsk, 107 members of Yorks/1 VAD men's detachments conveyed 1,558 patients, principally from East Leeds Military hospital where the seriously injured had been treated to most of the 32 auxiliary hospitals in the North Riding to convalesce. Others were taken to Harrogate, Hull, Wakefield and Ilkley.

Orderlies also met wounded men at Thirsk station, taking them to the hospital in Thirsk Town Hall by motor ambulances and "other conveyances".

By the end of 1919 The British Red Cross Society in the North Riding owned 12 ambulances including two belonging to Mrs Edward Shaw of Welburn Hospital, Kirbymoorside who placed them at the disposal of the Red Cross.

They were all distributed throughout the county for the use of civilians, soldiers and sailors as needed at the end of the war. Little wonder that after all this travelling, the soldiers were so relieved to reach the safety and calm of the Auxiliary Hospitals and extremely appreciative of the care and comfort that they received in them!

A TRIBUTE TO THE

R.O.D., R.E.

You ask what was the *R.O.D., lad,
　　To you it's only a name;
For we gained no distinction as heroes,
　　But we did our bit just the same.

We were mentioned now and then in dispatches
　　For duties we did under fire,
And we never asked for honours,
　　For honours we did not aspire.

We were mocked at as Fred Karno's Army,
　　But that never troubled us a bit,
We did our best for our Country,
　　In a manner our Country thought fit.

For the R.O.D. carried munitions,
　　We transported the men and the guns,
And kept our armies supplied, lad,
　　Whilst they were strafing the Huns.

We knew we were helping Great Britian,
　　Though we were not out to kill,
Willing to sacrifice life and limb,
　　To give her the best of our skill.

And if you look at the Roll of Honour
　　There you will plainly see,
That many a man died for his Country,
Though he served in the R.O.D.

*Railway Orderly Department.

The Hospital Ship, The Rohilla

The hospital ship, The Rohilla was sailing down the East coast on its way to Dunkirk to pick up wounded soldiers when, in the early hours of October 29th 1914 it struck the rocks at Saltwick Nab off Whitby. The lights of the warning buoy were extinguished because of the danger of enemy invasion, and there was a ferocious storm blowing.

The ship had been requisitioned by the Admiralty, and registered with the Red Cross. It was equipped as a hospital ship with two operating theatres and X-Ray equipment and nurses, doctors and sick berth attenders were on board.

On impact, the ship was broken in two, and all but one of the forty boats on board were smashed by the huge seas. The Rocket Brigade members made valiant efforts to send a line to the stricken ship, but it was beyond reach. The Whitby Lifeboat succeeded in rescuing thirty five people in two journeys, before being itself too damaged to be launched again.

Among the first to be saved were the five women on board, four nurses, and the stewardess, Mrs. Kezia Roberts, who had previously survived the sinking of The Titanic.

Superhuman efforts to reach the ship were made by Lifeboat crews from Scarborough, Upgang, and Redcar as local people watched helplessly from the cliff tops. It was not until fifty hours later that the motorised Lifeboat from Tynemouth, having made a hazardous nine hour journey overnight, was able to rescue the fifty people still clinging to the wreckage.

Of the two hundred and twenty nine people on board, one hundred and forty five were saved. Local people took the exhausted and injured survivors into their homes to provide warmth and comfort. Members of the British Red Cross and the Order of St. John helped to care for the bodies of those who had been killed.

Troopship "Rohilla"

Among those lost were twelve of the fifteen men of the Barnoldswick ambulance detachment who had volunteered as sick berth attenders. The bravery of the crews of the Lifeboats and the trawlers which had acted as tugs was recognised by awards from the Royal National Lifeboat Institute, and by the Admiralty.

A memorial bearing the names of the men who lost their lives stands in the cemetery in Whitby.

Medical Treatment

"Goals are to maintain fighter strength and soldier morale, assuage the angst of citizens unwilling to accept the human cost of war, and meet a moral obligation to the wounded warriors."

Numerous medical conditions were presented to the doctors and nurses in the hospitals during the war. Apart from obvious war wounds soldiers still suffered from more everyday conditions such as myalgia, nephritis, hernias, goitre, rheumatism and sleep disorders. Infection was a major issue in an era before penicillin had been discovered. Soldiers were more likely to die of infection than wounds themselves. In fact it is thought that half of the soldiers' deaths in Italy and Greece were due to illness rather than wounds.

It was reported in the War Illustrated Journal of 1917 that "every French soldier went into the war equipped with a little tincture of iodine in a glass vessel which he could break to spread this safe antiseptic over his own or his comrade's wound at the slightest possible notice. Our men are now so provided."

Wound Care.

Timely treatment and cleanliness were of the utmost importance when dealing with wounds. This is not easy to achieve in the battlefield. Over 41,000 men had their limbs amputated during World War 1, some due to the severity of the wound but others due to infection. A third of deaths were due to infection. Initially wounds could be flushed with boiled water with a few drops of carbolic or boric acid dissolved in the water.

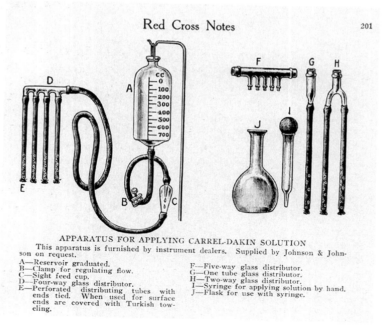

Red Cross Notes   201

APPARATUS FOR APPLYING CARREL-DAKIN SOLUTION
This apparatus is furnished by instrument dealers. Supplied by Johnson & Johnson on request.

A—Reservoir graduated.
B—Clamp for regulating flow.
C—Sight feed cup.
D—Four-way glass distributor.
E—Perforated distributing tubes with ends tied. When used for surface ends are covered with Turkish toweling.

F—Five-way glass distributor.
G—One tube glass distributor.
H—Two-way glass distributor.
I—Syringe for applying solution by hand.
J—Flask for use with syringe.

Permanganate of potash crystals could be added which took on the colour of "light claret". Izal (1 part to 800 parts boiled water) had the advantage of killing germs and was also cheap.

If none of these were available salt, turpentine, vinegar or methylated spirits could all be employed but was probably extremely painful for the soldiers. The second part of the treatment involved applying a clean dressing. Clean lint or linen was dipped in antiseptic, covered with oiled silk and then bandaged. The use of sphagnum moss was another treatment. The moss was picked in the North Riding (amongst other places) from where it was sent to a factory in York to be cleaned and compressed into a very absorbent dressing. It was sometimes combined with garlic to increase its antiseptic properties.

At its peak, Britain was manufacturing 1 million sphagnum moss bandages per month. By 1916 it was estimated that each soldiers' wound required at least 30 medical dressings.

The third part of the treatment was to rest, keeping the area still, which obviously might not happen until the soldiers were in the safer confines of a hospital. As the war progressed some doctors realised that the removal of all the dead tissue and dirt which could lead to infection was more effective.

If infection did occur in wounds gas gangrene could develop. This is a life threatening deadly form of gangrene due to clostridium and other soil borne bacteria. The area becomes very swollen and discoloured with large blisters. The smell of these wounds is very distinctive and unpleasant and was often mentioned by the nurses looking after these patients.

One of the major medical advances of the war was the use of the Carrel-Dakin method of treating wounds which was based on intermittent irrigating of the wounds with Dakins solution. Alexis Carrell was a French surgeon and biologist (1873 – 1944) who was awarded the Legion d'Honneur for his work on this subject. Henry Drysdale Dakin (1880 – 1852) an English chemist, born in Leeds, formulated Dakins solution. This solution was made up of sodium hypochlorite 0.4% and boric acid 4%. It was an unstable solution and deteriorated within a few days so was made up as required. It was useful because carbolic acid and iodine can lose their effect when blood serum is present.

Ursula Lascelles, a VAD nurse at Swinton Grange in the North Riding describes in her pocket book the use of Lotio Rubra which was an application of zinc sulphate and lavender water which breaks down granulations around wounds.

Nephritis (Bright's Disease)
Kidney infections were common amongst the soldiers which is probably not surprising given the damp conditions, the lack of toilet facilities and poor diet experienced in the war zones.

Signs and symptoms included headache, backache, feeling chilled, diarrhoea and vomiting and furred tongue. Soldiers' temperatures fluctuated from one extreme to another.

Treatment

Ursula Lascelles again described how soldiers must be kept warm and fed on a diet of milk and fish as well as having their urine measured and tested.

This is reinforced in "The Modern Physician 1911" which says that patients should be "clothed in flannel and placed in bed between blankets until the symptoms disappear". The diet was almost exclusively of milk which could be diluted to help its digestion. Chicken broth was also given and sometimes sodium bicarbonate and potassium citrate powders would be added to milk to concentrate the acidity of the milk. Plenty of water and occasionally barley water would be given to drink.

Frequent hot baths were required (temp 104 degrees F for 30-60 minutes) followed by being rubbed dry vigorously and rolled in warm sheets and blankets for 2-3 hours to encourage perspiration. This was believed to promote actions of skin in excretion of fluids, thus resting the kidneys. Saline purgatives could be given to promote bowel actions. Finally, warm poultices were applied to draw blood away from the kidneys and to relieve congestion.

Typhoid Fever

Treatment for typhoid fever was absolute rest and liquid diet only. Peptonised milk, beef tea, soups and beaten eggs formed the basis of nutrition followed by fish and boiled chicken as improvement was maintained. Urine and faeces had to be disinfected with izal then buried rather than put down drains to prevent the spread of infection.

Pneumonia

Treatment consisted of bed rest, tepid sponging, milk diet, water and lemonade to drink, and hot linseed meal poultice to counteract the pain. One of the complications was the development of heart failure so stimulants to strengthen the heart, such as alcohol, in moderation, were given.

Shell shock

"Not all war wounds are visible. Each major war has left a signature constellation of symptoms or neuroses called "shellshock" during World War 1 and referred to as PTSD (Post Traumatic Stress Disorder) in more recent times. The physiological, biochemical, and psychological causes and manifestations continue to be poorly understood and a great deal of controversy surrounds this subject"

Around 25% of all discharges in World War 1 were labelled "psychiatric casualties".

Signs and Symptoms
These were not specific but soldiers complained of affected sight, sound, smell and taste. Some were inexplicably paralyzed or were struck dumb. Others experienced uncontrollable tremors or had amnesia. They were exhausted and "war worn" and often emotional.

"Soldiers' Heart" or Da Costa's Syndrome describes a syndrome with symptoms of heart disease such as palpitations, fatigue, shortness of breath but with no physiological abnormalities noted on examination. It was thought to be a manifestation of an anxiety disorder and was treated as such.

There was a tendency for medical officers to appear unsympathetic as the emphasis on returning soldiers back to the war as quickly as possible meant they saw the men as malingerers.

Treatment
The early treatment was isolation, bed rest, massage and milk diet. However after more studies were done some doctors experimented with relaxation therapy, including the controlled use of rum.

Hypnosis was also used. Psychoanalysis, where soldiers were encouraged to talk about their fears and feelings, took place at certain hospitals and from these the early concept of counselling therapy was established. This combined with occupational therapy where soldiers performed light duties in kitchens, gardens or farms had a much better success rate than the earlier more extreme treatments.

Trench Foot
This term has been applied to the condition where soldiers developed painful and swollen feet due to immersion in cold water. This was prevalent in the trenches particularly during the winter months. It was occasionally called "frostbite" by some but realistically could have been called "water bite".

Trench foot developed because there was inertia of the muscles which led to a slowing down of the blood circulation. This attacked men who stood around in the trenches for long periods of time. If they were exercising vigorously or their feet were in constant motion they were less likely to suffer from trench foot.

Signs and Symptoms
Pain in the foot after initial numbness. The foot may appear blue in colour due to poor circulation but there may also be a red rash accompanied by swelling. In some cases small blisters formed and, less commonly, gangrene of the toes or of the skin surface occurred.

Treatment

Bed rest with the application of an evaporating lotion such as alcohol, was the best early treatment. Some doctors used a lead and opium wash and then later in the treatment exposed the area to the air. Gentle massage with olive oil and occasionally whale oil helped to lessen the symptoms.

Prophylaxis

As with all medical treatment, prevention is better than cure. The War Office issued a

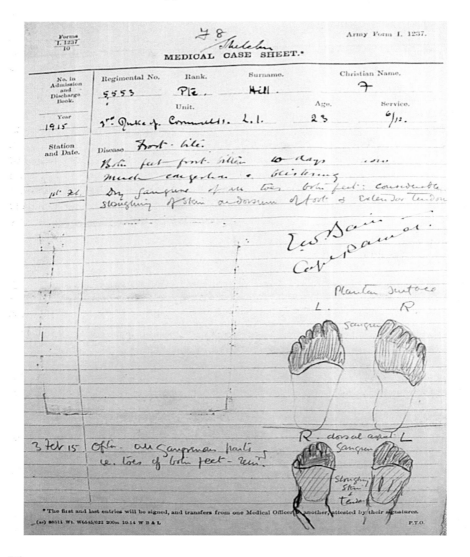

memorandum to the troops which advised:

1. Boots should not fit tightly, but should be at least a size too large. When boots are large enough it is well to wear two pairs of socks; but this is dangerous if the boots are small as this leads to further pressures on the feet. But these should never be applied tightly.
2. The general circulation can be kept up by keeping the body warm and dry. A mackintosh sheet worn over the great-coat is of assistance where no waterproof is available.
3. A dry pair of socks should be carried in the pockets when available.
4. Boots and puttees should be taken off at least once in twenty four hours, the feet rubbed and dried and a dry pair of socks put on.
5. Boots should be well greased or dubbined. Officers should see that dry standing is provided in the trenches wherever possible, by means of drainage, raising of the foot level by fascines of brushwood or straw with boards on top or by the use of pumps when these are available."

Trench Fever

Trench fever was discovered in 1915 and disappeared in 1918 at the end of the war but it did reappear in the Second World War. It is thought that it may have affected some 800,000 allied soldiers in World War 1. It has been described as a "disease of squalor". It had been thought that the disease was transmitted by the whole blood and was probably carried by "common flies or parasites found in the trenches". The louse was not identified as the vector until after the war. Trench conditions were ideal for the spread of disease with soldiers living in them for long periods of time surrounded by faeces, urine and dead bodies.

Signs and Symptoms

These included sudden onset of severe headaches, dizziness, muscular pains particularly in the legs and lumbar areas, high fever and chronic exhaustion. There was sometimes a rash. Constipation was also common and there were several relapses before the illness finally subsided. However, once it subsided, depression was a common complication.

Treatment

Bed rest, good diet and fluids and observation were the principle necessities for recovery. Commonly, infected soldiers were unfit for duty for three months as relapses caused return of five day bouts of infection.

After the war, the body louse was eventually identified as the culprit. The body louse became infected by feeding on the blood of the infected soldiers and then passed this onto a new host by biting them. Soldiers also scratched skin which was contaminated by louse excreta.

Lice often bed down in seams of clothing and there are descriptions of VAD nurses inspecting the seams of their aprons and dresses after they had finished their duties to physically remove them from their clothing!

On a positive note, some commentators have said that the toll of war dead would have been a lot higher if the lice had not infected so many men and interrupted their war service.

Gas

Many soldiers were affected by gassing. Chlorine was the first gas to be used and originally was used as a smokescreen rather than to kill. But it did kill or severely affect eye sight. Later mustard gas and phosgene were used, which attacked the respiratory system.

Medical Advances

Several medical triumphs were achieved during the war. These included antitoxin treatment of typhoid and tetanus, new methods of irrigating wounds, advances in the study of heart disease, rheumatism and dysentery, and plastic surgery. Plastic surgery of the face particularly made significant progress.

Once discoveries were made about the prevention of blood clotting by adding sodium citrate solution, blood transfusion was practised at the Front and no doubt saved many lives. It was common for other soldiers or members of staff to donate blood.

Mobile X-Ray units were first used in the war setting, enabling quicker diagnoses. Chloroform was used as an anaesthetic agent once it was transferred over to the battlefields. Some nurses were trained in its application and were then able to free the doctors to perform more surgery.

By 1916 80% of people with fractured femurs survived by being nursed in a Thomas Splint, a traction splint introduced in 1916.

There is no doubt that military hospitals demonstrated the "full range of bewildering choices and moral dilemmas that confront those charged with the delivery of medical care during war time."

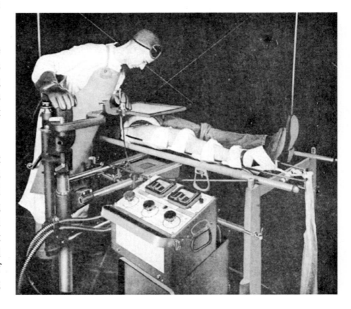

Fundraising

The immediate need for substantial funds was recognised by the British Red Cross as soon as war was declared. In the North Riding members paid a subscription of £5. 5s 0d and Associates £1.1s. 0d. Along with donations received a total of £387. 10s. 9d was raised.

In 1914 it was decided to ask churches of all denominations to make collections on a given date with a total of £68,000 being donated throughout the country in 1916. The previous year saw £1.2s.0d being donated by Finghall church, £1 by Nether Silton, 18s from Romanby, £6. 11s. 0d from All Saints Northallerton, and £14. 5s. 8d by St. Hilda's church, Middlesbrough.

The "Our Day" appeal launched in 1915 raised £1,036,789 nationally, and being so successful it was decided to continue it each year in October. The people of the North Riding held Whist Drives, Sales of Work, concerts and collections. Organ recitals by Rev. Father Calvert in Leyburn raised £1. 10s. 0d, the children of Bishopdale School in Aysgarth collected £5. 4s. 0d. and a rummage sale at Cloughton raised £29. 14s. 0d. In Pickering two fat stock sales in December led to a total of £60. 6s. 6d being donated, whilst in Swinton the sale of a pig brought in £25. 13s 0d.

The total donated to "Our Day" in 1917 in the North Riding amounted to £4,464. 10s. 4d., largely due to the efforts of a group of dedicated ladies. In 1918 this sum had risen to £7,623. 13s. 9d and a further £7,750. 1s 3d was received in donations.

The Alexandra Rose Day Collection had been started in 1912 to celebrate the 50th anniversary of the Princess Alexandra's arrival from Denmark. The Dowager Queen was keen that a scheme should be created to help the sick and needy by selling artificial wild roses which had been made by people with disabilities.

33

The first collection in the North Riding was held in 1918, when £2,636. 19s. 11d was raised, of which £ 1,479.13s. 6d. was to benefit local hospitals.

Expenses
In the 1917 Annual Report, the County Director, Major R.L. Bower stated that "In most cases the whole cost of preparation and equipment of hospitals has been borne by the locality concerned,"

All the hospitals, with the exception of Ayton Firs, Mulgrave Castle, Swinton Grange and Duncombe Park, which were organised and maintained at the owners' expense, received a grant of 3s. 3d. per occupied bed per day plus an unoccupied bed grant of 6d per day. Despite generous donations of beds, bedding, kitchenware, crockery and cutlery from local people, the cost of running the hospitals was considerable.

The upkeep of the Priory Hospital in Middleham with 12 beds was recorded as £78. 5s. 11d for the period between mid October and the end of December. At Baldersby Park, with 25 beds, expenditure from mid June to the end of the year was £460. 9s. 3d. During 1915 in Bedale Hall £788. 4s. 6d was spent on food, fires and lighting as well as medicines and dressings. In Richmond the bill for provisions came to £624.14s.8d, domestic needs £230.13s.5d and surgery and dispensary £91.0s.10d. Linen at Constable Burton Hospital cost £10. 4s. 0d whilst at Wykeham Abbey a water bed cost £4.

Money was also needed to buy clothes for men who were being discharged from hospital. Aysgarth and Constable Burton spent almost £11 on grey flannel shirting, flannel and wool to clothe the men leaving their care. A regular expense was the cost of travel for the V.A.D.s to attend training and tests in Northallerton, the fare by train from Sleights being 3/7 each. Meetings, lectures, telegrams and stationery all had to be paid for, as well as fees for the "boys for bandaging" practice and the doctor's fee for lectures.

Funds for overseas.
In addition to the continuing support for "Our Day", "Alexandra Rose Collection", church collections, and the local hospitals, the public were contributing donations to other national and international appeals.

In Swinton and Slingsby area money was sent to the Belgian Soldiers fund for food, clothes and hospital equipment, as well as to the Russian Prisoners of War Help Committee, to Holland to buy clothes, to the National Institute for the Blind, and to the Fund for British Prisoners of war in Germany. This organisation sent out parcels containing socks, hankies, towels, soap, plasters, zinc ointment, books, needles and cotton, cigarettes and verbena and lavendar.

In Northallerton, Mr. and Mrs. Weston Adamson organised a carnival at Mount Pleasant, (later known as the Mount and used as a Maternity Hospital), raising £800 of which £100 was donated to the Fund for Seamen.

Zeppelins help" Our Day" funds.

Throughout 1915 twenty Zeppelin raids had dropped 37 tons of bombs on Britain, resulting in 181 deaths and 455 people wounded. Hull was first attacked on 6th June 1915, leaving 40 people injured and 19 were killed. In May 1916 eighteen bombs were dropped on York in a Zeppelin raid killing a man and his wife, and London and other cities in the Eastern part of the country were targeted, at a cost of 293 civilian lives.

The Skelton Parish records state:

"Notice has been given to all households by the police that in the case of German Airships being reported by the telephone to the police as coming in our direction the church bells will be rung two or more together, making a clanging sound, also the mine hooters will give an intermittent sound, e.g. two short blasts followed by a long one means the same thing. On hearing either of these signals people are advised to go into the lower rooms of their homes. It is unwise to go into the street as a house will not protect you from a bomb, but it will protect against pieces of a bomb, which are dangerous from a very considerable distance."

On the night of September 2nd – 3rd 1916 the first airship was shot down over England, proving to be a turning point in the battle against them. The pilot, 2nd Lieutenant Leefe – Robinson of 39 (Home Defence) Squadron brought the Zeppelin plunging to earth in flames at the village of Cuffley in Hertfordshire. He was awarded the Victoria Cross for his achievement.

The event was greatly celebrated and the British Red Cross received 3 tons of the wire from the wreckage, which was cut into one inch lengths and sold for one shilling in an official envelope to raise funds as part of the "Our Day" efforts.

GUARANTEE.

This is a piece of the wire of the first Zeppelin brought down at CUFFLEY, HERTS. September 3rd, 1916. The wire having been given to the British Red Cross Society by H. M. War Office, it is being sold to help the wounded at the front.

Price 1/-

All in a Day's Work

"Girls who had never done anything more strenuous in their lives than put up their hair and pour the tea in drawing rooms pleaded with hospitals to let them scrub wards, feed patients and take temperatures"

The requirements for a V.A.D. nurse were that they were "presentable", had a reference from a doctor, priest or a magistrate, and that they were able to give time on a regular basis. In Military Hospitals, V.A.D.s had to be aged between 23 and 38, although in August 1918 this was extended to 21 to 48. It was not uncommon, however for younger women to start working as V.A.D.s in the Auxiliary Hospitals.

After completing a two week probationary period they were expected to serve for a minimum of three months, but many, in fact, served for the duration of the war. If they were found to be unsuitable in any way, however, their voluntary service could be terminated at any time.

The message to V.A.D.s proceeding on active service from Katharine Furse, Commandant in Chief, British Red Cross Society Women's Voluntary Aid Detachments, which was to be kept in their pocket books advised,

> DON'T talk about anything you hear in Hospital.
> DON'T criticise anybody, but do all you can to see that your own bit of work needs no criticism.
> DON'T forget you are under Military discipline – therefore under absolute obedience to all seniors.
> DON'T forget to stand up when seniors come into the ward or room.
> DON'T forget that when in uniform all members should be immaculately clean, trim and tidy.
> DON'T forget that outside public often judge the Association by the individual members.
> DON'T forget that duty comes before pleasure.
> DON'T expect your own particular likes or feelings to be considered. You are but one of many.
> DON'T think you can pick and choose your own work at first. Do all that comes your way with your whole heart, and others will see what you are best fitted for.
> DON'T forget to "Bring will to your work, and suit your mind to your circumstances – for that which is not for the interest of the whole swarm is not for the interest of the single bee! "(Marcus Aurelius.)

Their personal hygiene routine was to include twice daily gargling with carbolic 1 in 60; Listerine 1 tsp. to 5 0zs. water; Glyco Thymaline and water; combing their hair with a small tooth comb each night, and keeping their hands well washed and greased at night.

Katharine Furse wrote to the first V.A.D.s going to work overseas in 1915, "You are being sent to work for the Red Cross. You have to perform a task which will require your courage, your energy, your patience, your humility, your determination to overcome all difficulties. Remember that the honour of the V.A.D. organisation depends on your individual conduct. It will be your duty not only to set an example of discipline and perfect steadiness of character, but also to maintain the most courteous relations with those whom you are helping in this great struggle.

Be invariably courteous, unselfish and kind. Remember, whatever duty you undertake, you must carry it out faithfully, loyally, and to the best of your ability.

Rules and regulations are necessary in whatever formation you join. Comply with them without grumble or criticism and try to believe there is a reason at the back of them, though at the time you may not understand the necessity. Sacrifices may be asked of you. Give generously and wholeheartedly, grudging nothing, but remembering that you are giving because your Country needs your help. If you see others in better circumstances than yourself, be patient and think of the men who are fighting amid discomfort and who are often in great pain.

Those of you who are paid can give to the Red Cross Society which is your Mother and which needs much more money to carry on its great work to their Mother Society and thus to the Sick and Wounded. Let our mottos be "Willing to do anything" and "The People give gladly". If we live up to these, the V.A.D. members will come out of this triumphant."

Training
All V.A.D.s had to complete the courses in Home Nursing and in First Aid as set out by the British Red Cross and the Order of St. John.

The courses were often tutored by the local family doctor, and boys from the Scout group acted as patients for practicing bandaging. On passing the examination the V.A.D.s were given a certificate, as well as a medal, with bars to be added for each successive year.

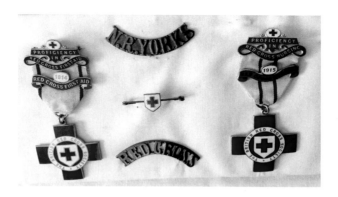

Members also attended training at Field Days, held annually in Northallerton and other locations. Training was maintained and tested as illustrated in the report of the North Riding Branch of June 1914.

"The third Field Day of North Riding Branch took place at Northallerton where work done and the Detachment were inspected by Major - General Sir John S. Cowans K.C.B. N.V.O. (Quartermaster General of the Forces) and Surgeon General Kenny C.D.D.M.S. Northern Command. Detachments paraded and competitions were held in First Aid to the wounded, organising and improvising hospitals, pitching tents, improvising Ambulance wagons, transporting the wounded, and field cooking."

Uniforms

The outdoor uniform for V.A.D.s was a long navy blue single breasted great coat and a distinctive large brimmed hat with a metal Red Cross badge. The indoor uniform which was bought by the V.A.D. cost £1. 19s. 2½d. It consisted of a loose fitting long blue dress with full length sleeves, starched collar, sleeves, and apron, and the traditional 'Dora' cap which was later replaced with the plain white veil. Black stockings and shoes completed the outfit. The red cross was made and sown on to the apron by the V.A.D.s themselves. Donations received from the public helped to pay for the other requirements which included:

        Surgical scissors 2 shillings
        Forceps 1/9d
        Probe 1s
        Flannel for bandages 1/8d
        Safety pins 6d
        Muslin and tape 1s
        Oxide Zinc plasters 2s
        Health salts 6½d

V.A.D.s were advised to wear British Red Cross armbands and to carry a Certificate of Identity as the emblem entitled the wearer to international protection in the event of an invasion, and it was also proof that they were trained in first Aid which would be useful in an emergency.

Discipline

In the Annual Report 1915 Major R.F. Ruck Keene, the County Director of the North Riding wrote;
"The observance of discipline in a hospital whether in peace or war, is an obligation both for staff and patients, and it is really wonderful how readily the Detachments have adapted themselves to the conditions of which they had no previous experience. The result has been excellent. But it cannot however be too frequently impressed on all that discipline and loyalty, even in the smallest matters, must go hand in hand, regardless of any personal considerations."

In 'The Way Of The Red Cross' published in 1915 to raise funds for 'Our Day', "It is one of the rules of the conduct of the Society that all work shall be purely voluntary and it is one of the triumphs of the Red Cross organisation and work that voluntary workers have so willingly submitted to discipline."

Members of the nursing profession and members of the public objected to the use of the title "nurse" for the V.A.Ds who had, at the outbreak of war, minimal training and little experience, whilst earning handsome medals and certificates for their efforts.

Nevertheless, as the war continued the V.A.D.s proved their worth by developing competence and maturity in all the fields of work which were demanded of them, and their nursing colleagues grew to respect and value their contribution.

The British Red Cross North Riding Report 1915;
"Because of the demand for trained nurses at the Front V.A.D.s were especially selected by the V.A. Selection Board at Devonshire House, London to nurse in Hospitals overseas. In 1915, 80 V.A.D.s volunteered from the North Riding, of whom 18 have so far been posted to Hospitals leaving 15 at present on the accepted list". By 1918 this number had increased to 608 V.A.D.s applying, 499 being posted in Hospitals.
Having gained skills and experience some V.A.D.s extended their training to practice as anaesthetists to enable the medical staff to cope with their ever increasing work load. Lady D'Abernon, of Duncombe Park was proud of having administered 1,137 anaesthetics without losing any patients.

Other V.A.D.s were successful in the "Blue Stripe Examination for Efficiency" to qualify as V.A.D. Assistant Nurses.

Day To Day Routine

Initially it was intended that V.A.D.s should do the work of orderlies, including cleaning, bed making, feeding the men, giving them blanket baths, and taking their temperatures. For young women who had a limited experience of life and men, giving such personal care could be daunting. Although the V.A.D.s often referred to the soldiers as "their boys", and in turn, the men had affectionate nicknames for them such as "very adorable darlings", the balance of warm, compassionate care and professional detachment had to be struck.

The day began with assisting the patients to rise, wash and shave before breakfast. The men who were up and about, officially referred to as the "Up patients", but generally known as the "bluebirds" were expected to help with tasks around the ward.

The 'Up' patients were given an ill fitting blue suit (known as a 'bluey') to wear, which had wide white lapels and was worn with a red tie, slippers when inside, and their boots when they went out. This was issued in the early part of the war, as previously, when wearing their military uniform, men had been insulted and shown the white feather by local people not realising that they were convalescing from their injuries and illnesses. Men confined to bed wore nightshirts, often made by local work parties and donated to the hospitals. The round by the Medical Officer and Matron started at 9a.m., by which time the ward and the patients had to be clean and tidy.

Treatments were then given and dressings changed. Dressing the men's wounds was a major part of the work, taking considerable time and care. The procedure was often extremely painful for the men, and put the nurses or V.A.D.s at significant risk of infection. Only nurses were allowed to use protective gloves, so others had to rely on scrupulous handwashing and use of disinfectant to dip their hands in after dressings were completed.

When conventional dressings were in short supply, Sphagnum moss was used to make highly absorbent, soft, antiseptic pads. The moss had been collected from the local countryside, cleaned at the depot in York, then dried and formed into pads in muslin. To enhance its' natural antiseptic properties, garlic juice was squeezed over the dressing, which was then said to be able to absorb twenty times its' own weight.

To A RED CROSS NURSE.

DEAR NURSE THE GRATITUDE & THANKS
OF MANY FELLOWS IN THE RANKS
FOR ALL YOUR CARE AND SKILL ARE DUE,
SOME OF US OWE OUR LIVES TO YOU,
AND SO THIS LITTLE SOUVENIR
COMES WISHING YOU THE BEST OF CHEER.

Poultices were used to convey heat and moisture to the skin as long as it was unbroken. This relieved pain, and was thought to disperse inflammation and hasten the formation of pus, important in the fight against infection before antibiotics were invented. Linseed, charcoal, bran, starch, oatmeal and sugar were all used to make poultices. Bread poultices were helpful for injuries to the face, neck or head as it was light and did not smell. A thick slice of bread with the crusts removed was placed on a clean handkerchief or piece of linen and boiling water or milk was poured over it. It was then ready for use but the poultice needed to be well covered and was to be changed after four hours or when it was cold.

Bran poultices were thought to be beneficial for sprains, rheumatic pain, and neuralgia. The "congestion of the lungs", caused by chest infections and pneumonia which were common complications of the injuries sustained, could be relieved by inhaling steam directly from a Nelson's inhaler, with the patient's head swathed in a towel to create a tent. The V.A.D. was responsible for distributing the inhalers twice a day and keeping them topped up with hot water whilst in use.

Other duties included the emptying of the sputum pots, bedpans and urinals of the men who were bed bound, helping them to eat and drink, and supporting them when they were able to get out of bed. Masseuses, some of whom were members of the Almeric-Paget Massage Corps were employed in the hospitals, including those in Crathorne Hall, Masham Town Hall, Wykeham Abbey and Welburn Hall. At Duncombe Park Miss Mathilde Bengtsson, holder of the Diploma of the Royal Institute of Medical Gymnastics and Massage from Stockholm, was employed.

Massage was recognised as a most important technique for restoring strength and function to damaged muscles. The V.A.D.s who were interviewed later about their work had memories of how important it had been to comfort and sustain the men by touch, just by holding their hands in times of distress. The men whose eyesight had been affected by gassing were also appreciative of the V.A.D.s writing letters home for them and reading their post when it arrived.

The days could be long and painful for the men, and the V.A.D.s went to great efforts to occupy and entertain them. Most hospitals had a snooker table and a gramophone. The local communities donated jigsaws, books and board games, organised trips to theatres and concerts, and arranged sports contests. However the Defence Of the Realm Act prohibited the men from visiting public houses, or even being given any alcohol, other than for medicinal purposes.

Animals too were part of the rehabilitation of the men and there are many photos which include the pets of the owners of the hospital. Flowers from the gardens and countryside were used to decorate the wards, and sweets and cigarettes were bought by the V.A.D.s for "their boys".

In this holistic care of body and mind, the men's spiritual needs were not neglected. At Duncombe Park, prayers were taken in the private chapel on Monday and Wednesday evenings, and there were occasional Sunday services. Some patients were confirmed by the Bishop of Beverley in the private chapel in April 1916. The monks from Ampleforth Abbey took a great interest in the hospitals, visiting soldiers of the Roman Catholic faith.

V.A.D.

THERE's an angel in our ward as keeps a-flittin' to and fro
With fifty eyes upon 'er wherever she may go;
She's as pretty as a picture and as bright as mercury,
And she wears the cap and apron of a V.A.D.

The Matron she is gracious and the Sister she is kind,
But they wasn't born just yesterday and lets you know
    their mind;
The M.O. and the Padre is as thoughtful as can be,
But they ain't so good to look at as our V.A.D.

She's a honourable miss because 'er father is a dook,
But, Lord, you'd never guess it and it ain't no good to look
For 'er portrait in the illustrated papers, for you see
She ain't an advertiser, not *our* V.A.D.

Not like them that wash a tea-cup in an orficer's canteen
And then "Engaged in War Work" in the weekly Press is
    seen;
She's on the trot from morn to night and busy as a bee,
And there's 'eaps of wounded Tommies bless that V.A.D.

She's the lightest 'and at dressin's and she polishes the
    floor,
She feeds Bill Smith who'll never never use 'is 'ands no
    more;
And we're all of us supporters of the harristocracy
'Cos our weary days are lightened by that V.A.D.

And when the War is over, some knight or belted earl,
What's survived from killin' Germans, will take 'er for 'is
    girl;
They'll go and see the pictures and then 'ave shrimps and
    tea;
'E's a lucky man as gets 'er—and don't I wish 'twas me!

Extract from Punch, August 13th 1917

Auxiliary Hospitals in the North Riding
1914 - 1919

10

List of Hospitals.

No.	Hospital.	Opened.	Commandant.	No. of Beds equipp'd	No. of patients treated.
1	Ayton Firs ...	15 Dec., '14	Mrs. A. E. Kitching ...	20	Now closed.
2	Bolton Hall ...	16 Oct., '14	The Lord Bolton ...	12	Now closed.
3	(Bedale Hall ...	1 Jan., '18	Lady Beresford-Peirse ...	50	350
	(Bedale Red Cross...	16 Oct., '14		30	
4	Baldersby Park ..	1 Feb., '15	Mrs. Brennand ...	26	Now closed.
5	Crathorne Hall ...	13 Nov., '14	Mrs. Lionel Dugdale ...	25	423
6	Cober Hill ...	15 Dec., '14	Dr. B. G. Forman ...	35	469
7	Constable Burton ...	16 Oct., '14	Mrs. D'arcy Wyvill ...	12	Now closed.
8	Danby Hall ...	16 Oct., '24	Mrs. Henry Scrope ...	10	Now closed.
9	Duncombe Park ..	28 June, '15	Lady Marjorie Beckett ..	36	293
10	Guisborough ...	15 Dec., '15	The Lady Holden of Alston	20	Now closed.
11	Hovingham Hall ...	4 Jan., '15	Dr. Smeeton ...	58	458
12	Masham ..	17 Jan., '18	The Lady Masham ...	40	16
13	Malton ...	22 Feb., '15	Miss Lupton ...	23	347
14	Middleham ...	16 Oct., '14	Mrs. Topham ...	12	Now closed.
15	Middlesbrough ...	25 Oct., '17	Mrs. Hedley ...	51	94
16	Mulgrave Castle ...	15 Dec., '14	Rev. The Marquis of Normanby	40	350
17	Northallerton ...	16 Oct., '14	Dr. Baigent ...	65	1167
18	Pickering ...	1 April, '15	Mrs. J. L. Kirk ...	22	243
19	Red Barnes, Redcar	9 Jan,, '15	Mrs. Claud Pease, O.B.E....	60	724
20	Richmond ...	16 Oct., '14	Miss E. Pease, O.B.E. ...	64	712
21	Rounton ...	13 Nov., '14	Lady Bell ...	37	234
22	Scarbro' Weston ...	Feb., 1915	Col. Hastings-Fowler ...	35	Now closed.
23	Saltburn ...	Jan., 1915	Miss Robertson ...	48	538
24	Skelton ...	1 April, '15	Dr. Burnett ...	36	1355
25	Sleights ...	Dec., 1914	Miss Yeoman, O.B.E. ...	26	292
26	Stanwick Park ...	Jan., 1915	Miss I. Wilson, O.B.E. ...	50	666
27	Stokesley ...	Dec., 1914	Mrs. Gjers ...	60	576
28	Swinton Grange ...	Sept., 1914	The Hon. Mrs. Behrens ...	23	524
29	Scorton	Dec., 1914	Dr. Phelps ...	25	Now closed.
30	Thirsk ...	Dec., 1914	Dr. Ferguson ...	65	667
31	Welburn Hall ...	June, 1916	Mrs. Ed. Shaw ...	50	129
32	Wydale, Brompton	Oct., 1914	Mr. P. Illingworth ...	15	Now closed.
33	Wykeham Abbey ...	Oct., 1914	The Hon. Norah Dawney...	70	1159

45

Ayton Firs Hospital, Great Ayton

"Ayton Firs" Hospital, Great Ayton.

Building lent by	Mr. and Mrs. Kitching.
Date of opening	December 10th, 1914.
Date of closing	November 11th, 1915.
No. of Beds	20.
Total No. of patients treated	50.
No. of deaths	None.
Hospital affiliated to	Military Hospital, York.
Commandant	Mrs. Kitching.
Medical Officer	Charles Stuart, Esq., M.B., Great Ayton.
Staffed by	Trained Nurses and private household staff.

This Hospital was organised and maintained by Mr. and Mrs. Kitching entirely at their own expense. It did an immense amount of good work during the first eighteen months of the war, when Hospital accommodation was so urgently needed.

Ayton Firs is believed to have been built between 1860 and 1877 for Mr Alfred Kitching, a local businessman who was involved with Whessoe Foundry and the establishment of the Darlington and Stockton Railway. His son Alfred Edward Kitching (1858-1938) lived in the house during the war years with his wife Annie who was a daughter of Joseph Richardson of Potto Hall. Alfred was a JP and a Deputy Lieutenant of the North Riding. Ayton Firs was one of the first houses in the area to have a telephone installed. Alfred and Annie's son Colonel Harold Edward Kitching was a rower for Great Britain in the 1908 Olympic Games. He saw service in WW1, being commissioned in the Durham Light Infantry in 1914. He was twice mentioned in despatches.

The hospital ward at Ayton Firs was set up in the ballroom of the house which had previously seen excitement at the "coming out" of the Kitching's daughter.
Today the house is divided into two separate privately owned dwellings.

WOUNDED AT GREAT AYTON.

Mrs A. E. Kitching and the wounded
soldiers at Ayton Firs Hospital beg to
acknowledge with grateful thanks the following kind presents:—Mr Worthy Pearson and customers, 307 cigars and 10oz
cigarettes; Mrs Charles Hodgson, 1 1oz
fresh eggs; Mrs Henry Kitching, shirts,
vests, nightshirts, socks, sleeping socks,
pillow cases, games, and apples; Mr Henry
Kitching, pipes, tobacco, and cigarettes;
Mrs Monkman, cigarettes; Mrs Wm.
Hutton, six foot warmers; maids at Ayton
Firs, knitted socks; maids at the Grange,
knitted socks; Mrs Ada Jackson, bananas;
Mrs Maitland, tobacco; Alice and
Arthur Sanderson, Gertie and Sydney
Wilson, cigarettes.

*Extract from The Middlesborough
Daily Gazette December 14th 1914.*

Other reports in the gazette:

18/9/14 It is reported that the Great Ayton branch of Queen Mary's Needlework
Guild provided 35 flannel night shirts, 12 linen night shirts, 22 pillowcases, 2 pairs
sheets, and 5 bed jackets.

15/10/14 The children of Marwood School Great Ayton subscribed weekly to a
school fund where the money is used to buy wool. The girls were knitting socks,
cholera belts, and mittens while the boys knitted mufflers!

23/12/14 Transport of wounded soldiers from York to be taken to Ayton Firs Hospital
was undertaken by a detachment of men from Great Ayton Ambulance Brigade using
horse drawn ambulances provided by Roseberry Mines.

31/12/14 A concert was held at Ayton Firs for the wounded soldiers, friends and staff
by Cleveland Glee Singers, who were given an "enthusiastic reception."

24/7/16 In an article "What the women of Thornaby are doing" it was reported that
Mrs Kitching of Ayton Firs presented badges and certificates to the members of Yorks
54 Women's VAD Detachment. She thanked the nurses for their energetic practical
work in the hospital, which was most appreciated.

The financial report for Great Ayton Red Cross in 1915 mentions expenditure on
ambulance rugs 5/6 each, stretcher £2-3s-6d, Red Cross haversacks £1-8s-6d and kit
bags for ambulance gear £2-17s-0d.

Commandant: Miss Miller.

Medical Officer: Dr. Tarleaton.

Name.	Record of War Service.	Part time or Whole time.
Miller, Miss Lilian R. ...	Commandant and Lady Superintendent. The Firs, Great Ayton ; Race Course, Cheltenham ; Holgate, Middlesbro'...	Part time
Spence, Mrs. Dorothea ...	Hon. Commandant ...	„
Welsh, Miss Annie ...	Quartermaster. The Firs, Gt. Ayton ; Racecourse, Chelten ham ; Holgate, Middlesbro' ..	„
Brittain, Miss Isabel ...	Holgate, Middlesbro' ...	„
Brown, Mrs. Margaret ...	„ „ ...	„
Chandler, Mrs. Sarah ...	„ „ ...	„
Hazelwood, Miss Ruth ...	The Firs, Gt. Ayton ; Holgate, Middlesbro' ..	„
Jenkins, Miss Alice ...	Holgate, Middlesbro' ..	„
McMurray, Mrs. Rhoda ...	„ „ ..	„
Robertson, Mrs. Jean ...	The Firs, Gt. Ayton ; Holgate, Middlesbro' ...	„
Robinson, Miss Mary ...	The Firs, Gt. Ayton ; Racecourse, Cheltenham ...	„
Rogers, Miss Annie ...	The Firs, Gt. Ayton ; R.A.M.C. at home ; R.A.M.C. Abroad	Whole time
Ransom, Miss Margaret ...	Holgate, Middlesbro' ..	Part time
Rhodes, Mrs. Florence ...	„ „	„
Ormerod, Miss Margaret ...	Queen Mary's, Roehampton ...	„
Ormerod, Miss Emily ...	„ „	„
Walker, Miss Bertha ...	Holgate, Middlesbro' ...	„
Wood, Miss Mary ...	„ „ ...	„
Crierie, Miss Doris ...	The Firs, Gt. Ayton ...	„

Registered on 9th December 1914, there were 24 members of the Yorks./31 VAD Men's Detachment with J. White Esq. as their Commandant. By 1918 though it was reported that there had not been any active work done in the last year. This may have been due to men being called up to serve in the army or taking on other war work.

A beautifully written roll of honour, held in Christ Church Great Ayton, commemorates all the men of the village who served in the war. It also includes a page with the names of three V.A.D. nurses, Joyce Fry, Elrie Dixon and Mary Wesley, although where they nursed has not been recorded in the details given in the British Red Cross minutes 1914-1919.

Baldersby Park Hospital

"Baldersby Park Hospital," Thirsk.		
Building lent by		Mrs. Brennand.
Date of opening	...	1st, 1915.
Date of closing		July 23rd, 1917.
No. of Beds ...	...	25.
Total number of patients treated ...	...	285.
No. of deaths ...	...	None.
Hospital affiliated to ...	.. East Leeds War Hospital.	
Commandant		... Mrs. Brennand.
Medical Officers		Dr. Talbot Mitchell.
		Dr. Guy C. Mitchell.
Quartermaster and Secretary ...		G. H. Peirson, Esq.
Staffed by ...	Yorks./64 and Trained Nurses.	

The house, originally known as Newby Park, was built in 1720 and was the earliest known example of an English neo- Palladian villa. The architect Colen Campbell designed it for Sir William Robinson (1655-1736). The spacious Georgian mansion was set in a 200 acre park which was well wooded and stocked with fallow deer.

George Hudson, the Railway King and Lord Mayor of York bought the house in 1845 but sold it to the 7th Viscount Downe in 1854. He changed its name to Baldersby Park to avoid confusion with Newby Hall. The house was sold again in 1900 to John Brennand who permitted its use as a hospital in WW1. John Brennand was the Sheriff

of Yorkshire for 1915-1916. His wife Katherine was the Commandant of the hospital and their daughter Nadine was a VAD nurse there. She was 27 years old at the onset of the war.

Having made their fortune in the cotton industry the Brennand family was ruined in the cotton market crash of 1927. The house and park were sold again to become Skellfield School for Girls. From 1985 to the present day it has been the home of Queen Mary's School for Girls.

Some of the following photos come from albums in the possession of the school.

Yorks./64. Baldersby.

Commandant : Mrs. Brennand.

Name.	Record of War Service.		Part time or Whole time.
Brennand, Mrs. Katherine ...	Baldersby Park Auxiliary	...	Whole time
Brennand, Miss Nadine ...	,, ,,	...	Whole time
Blakeborough, Mrs. Emily ...	,, ,,	...	Part time
Brown, Mrs. Katherine H. ...	,, ,,	...	,,
Brown, Mrs. Martha Ann ...	,, ,,	...	,,
Barley, Mrs. Henrietta ...	,, ,,	...	,,
Batty, Miss Christiana ...	,, ,,	...	,,
Dent, Miss Mary ...	,, ,,	...	,,
Franks, Miss Violet ...	,, ,,	...	,,
Hathsway, Mrs. Margaret Pattison ...	,, ,,	...	,,
Morton, Mrs. Sarah ...	,, ,,	...	,,
Potter, Miss Nellie ...	,, ,,	...	,,
Robinson, Mrs. Martha ...	,, ,,	...	,,
Richardson, Miss Gladys M. ...	,, ,,	...	,,
Stubbs, Miss Maud ...	,, ,,	...	,,
Stratford, Mrs. Isabella ...	,, ,,	...	,,
Stringer, Mrs. Sarah J. ...	,, ,,	...	,,
Lindsay, Miss Mary ...	,, ,,	...	,,
Duncan, Miss Ella ...	,, ,,	...	,,
Antrobus, Miss Lena ...	,, ,,	...	,,
I'Anson, Miss Nellie R. ...	,, ,,	...	,,
I'Anson, Miss Dorothy ...	,, ,,	...	,,

The Quartermaster and Secretary of the hospital was George Henry Pearson who was the land steward for Baldersby Park. The wife of the estate gardener, James Henry Hathaway was a VAD nurse. She was called Margaret Pattison Hathaway and was 36 at the beginning of the war. They had three daughters and all can be seen in this photo outside one of the greenhouses on the estate.

The teapot presented by the VAD nurses at Balderby to the cook at the hospital, Ada Norris on her marriage to the chauffeur and blacksmith, John Forrester. The couple later settled in Topcliffe.

A little boating on the lake for this soldier while others walk around the grounds in the distance.

Photo of the wounded soldiers' cricket team.
They played against the nurses' team. We do not know who won the match.

Two soldiers taking their
breakfast out into the garden.

Soldiers and nurses pose
outside the house.

Bedale Hall Red Cross Hospital

"Bedale Hall Red Cross Hospital," Bedale.

Building lent by	...	Sir Henry Beresford-Peirse, Bart.
Date of opening	... ...	October 29th, 1914.
Date of closing	... ...	February 28th, 1919.
No. of Beds ...	... ...	... 80.
Total number of patients treated	... ...	826.
No. of deaths	... ...	None.
Hospital affiliated to	... ...	Military Hospital, York.
Commandant	...	Lady Beresford-Peirse, O.B.E.
Medical Officer	...	... Dr. Alan Hansell, Bedale.
Quartermaster	... ...	Miss Maud Kirby.
Staffed by ...	...	Yorks./18 and Trained Nurses.

Now a Grade 1 listed building, Bedale Hall was the family home of Sir Henry and Lady Henrietta Beresford-Peirse who lent the building to be used as an Auxiliary Hospital throughout the war years.

Lady Beresford-Peirse was the District Representative and was also a member of County and Executive British Red Cross committees as well as an enthusiastic fund raiser for the " Our Day" collections and "Nation's Fund for Nurses" in 1918.

Sir Henry Beresford-Peirse served as the Chairman of the North Riding County Council during the war, and gave approval for improvements in the facilities for soldiers who were being nursed at County Hall, including a new cooking range and sink to be installed in the basement at the expense of the Red Cross.

The Chairman of the County Council reported that since the last quarterly Meeting of the Committee he had given permission for a bath, for the use of the Red Cross Hospital, to be put in the small upstairs room at the end of the South corridor, at the expense of the Red Cross ; and that he had sanctioned the use, by the wounded soldiers only, of the grounds at the South side of the County Hall for playing croquet and bowls.

H. BERESFORD-PEIRSE,
Chairman.

Northallerton, 12th July, 1915.

Yorks./18. Bedale.

Commandant : Lady Beresford Peirse, O.B.E.

Medical Officer - Dr. Alan Hansell.

Name.	Record of War Service.	Part time or Whole time.
Beresford-Peirse, Lady Henrietta	Commandant. Bedale Red Cross Hospital	Part time
Kirby, Miss Maud	Asst. Commandant.	Half time
Beresford-Peirse, Miss Mary	Quartermaster.	Part time
Hansell, Dr. Alan	Medical Officer.	
Thornton, Mr.	Pharmacist.	No duty
Ackroyd, Miss Catherine	Masham Red Cross Hospital	Part time
Abbott, Mrs. Mary	Bedale Red Cross Hospital	Occasional
Atkinson, Miss Catherine	Bedale and Masham Hospitals	Part time
Bell, Miss Mildred	Bedale Hospital	,,
Brown, Miss Catherine	,, ,,	,,
Courage, Mrs. Beatrice	,,	
Coore, Mrs. Evelyn	,, ,,	,,
Dobby, Miss Gertrude	,, ,,	,,
Dobby, Miss Annie	Bedale and Military Hospital, Catterick	,,
Deighton, Mrs. Annie Maude	Masham Hospital	,,
Eddison, Mrs. Constance	Bedale Hospital	,,
Edmundson, Miss Emma	Bedale and Masham Hospitals	,,
Edgar, Mrs. Margaret	,, ,,	,,
Fife, Mrs. Aileen	Bedale Hospital	,,
Fothergill, Miss Grace	Bedale, 13 months ; and 1st Northern Gen. Hosp., Newcastle-on-Tyne	,,
Fothergill, Miss Maud	Bedale, St. Thomas's, Rouen, and Roehampton	Whole & part
Gray, Miss Edith Cresswell	Bedale Hospital	Part time
Gray, Miss Irene Cresswell	,, ,,	,,
Gray, Miss Margarita Cresswell	,, ,,	,,
Gibson, Mrs. Elsie	,,	,,
Gent, Miss Ethel	Bedale and Masham	,,
Hood, Miss Margaret	Bedale Hospital	,,
Hare, Mrs. Margaret	,, ,,	,,
Halfpenny, Miss Maud	,, ,,	,,
Heywood, Miss Jane	,, ,,	,,
Ingleby, Miss Natalie	Bedale and Masham	,,
Kirby, Miss Rose	Bedale Hospital	,,
Learoyd, Miss Alice Nelson	,, ,,	,,
Linscott, Miss Elsie	,, ,,	,,
McDonie, Miss Harriet	,, ,,	,,
Musgrave, Miss Emily	,, ,,	,,
Maister, Miss Gladys	Masham Hospital	,,
McIntyre, Miss Ellen	Bedale Hospital	,,
McIntyre, Miss Josephine	,, ,,	,,

54

Name.	Record of War Service.	Part time or Whole time.
•Mace, Miss Alice ...	Bedale Hospital	Part time
Nicholson, Miss Florence ...	" "	"
Newton, Miss Harriet M. ...	Masham	"
Pearson, Miss Annie ...	Bedale Hospital	"
Peacock, Miss Rachel ...	" "	"
Pallin, Miss Greta ...	Bedale and Red Barns, Redcar	Whole time
Beresford-Peirse, Miss Dorothy	Bedale, Tunbridge Wells, and St. Dunstan's	Part time
Pinkney, Miss Edith .	Bedale	"
Park, Miss Margaret ...	Bedale, Saltburn, and Welburn Hall	"
Pattison, Mrs. Isabella ...	Bedale Hospital	"
Pauling, Miss Marie ...	General Hospital, London, Connaught Hospital, Aldershot ...	Whole time
Springett, Miss Guglielma ...	Bedale Hospital	Part time
Towler, Miss Milicent ...	" " .	"
Theakston, Miss Dora ...	Masham Hospital	"
Weeler, Mrs. Susan ...	"	"
Wood, Miss Cecil ...	Bedale	"
Whitton, Miss Mary ...	"	"
Whitton, Miss Annie ...	"	"
Wheldon, Miss Mary ...	"	"
Watson, Miss Ethel J. ...	Masham	"
Wandesforde, Miss Maud Prior	Bedale and The Grove, Harrogate	"
Wright, Miss Sarah ...	Bedale Hospital	"
Webster, Miss Dorothy Steer ...	Bedale and War Hospital, Dunstan, Northants	"

Lady Beresford-Peirse was the Commandant of the 43 strong women's Detachment Yorks/18 and Dr. Eddison, followed by Dr. Alan Waites Hansell led the Men's Detachment Yorks/17. Dr. Hansell was the local G.P. who also served as the Medical Officer for the hospital.

The V.A.D. fourth from left on the back row is Miss Margaret Park who later lived near the mill in Aiskew.

55

Miss Edie Pinkney, another V.A.D., later told her two daughters stories of her caring for the Belgian soldiers, and being taught how to enquire after the progress of one man's arm in French. Her husband, Sydney Bird, who had served in France, died when he was 37 years old, leaving Edie to bring up two very young girls with the help of her parents who ran a shop in Crakehall.

Mary and Annie Whitton were cousins of Margaret Park, all working as V.A.Ds at Bedale Hall. The drawing of Nan (? Annie) and the piece 'Bedale V.A.D.' are entries in the autograph album of Margaret, kindly lent by her niece, Mrs. Valerie Anderson.

The soldiers in the hospital were given treats by the owner of Suttells shop who made ice cream for them. The good care was obviously appreciated as expressed in these two entries in the autograph album from Belgian soldiers.

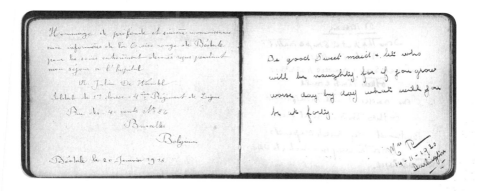

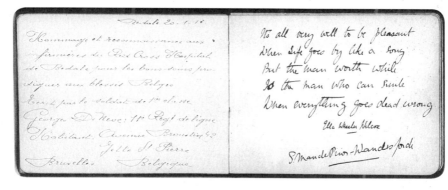

Bedale Red Cross Staff during the First World War.

Bolton Hall Red Cross Hospital

"Bolton Hall Hospital," Leyburn.

Building lent by	... ...	The Lord Bolton.
Date of opening	... ..	October 15th, 1914.
Date of closing	... ...	January 19th, 1915.
No. of Beds ...	... ...	.. ... 13.
Total number of patients treated	... ...	13.
No. of deaths	...	... None.
Hospital affiliated to	... ...	Military Hospital, York.
Commandant	... ...	The Lord Bolton.
Medical Officer	George Cockcroft, Esq., M.D., Middleham.	
Quartermaster	... ...	Miss Hawtayne.
Staffed by ...	...	Yorks./16 and Trained Nurses.

This small Hospital was opened in the early days of the War to meet the rush of Belgian wounded into this Country.

Bolton Hall, one of the Dales hospitals used at the beginning of the war to treat wounded Belgian soldiers, was only open for a short time.

Dr George Cockcroft, the local GP who acted as the medical officer of the hospital.

Yorks./16.   Constable Burton.

Commandant: Mrs. D'arcy Wyvill.

Medical Officer : Dr. Jas. Peacock.

Name.	Record of War Service.	Part time or Whole time.
Barclay, Lady Letitia	Bolton and Northallerton Hospitals	Part time
Beswick, Miss Maud	Northallerton	,,
Bosvile, Miss Helen	Bolton and Northallerton	,,
Bowes, Miss Helena	Bolton and Northallerton	,,
Broadley, Miss Margaret	Northallerton	
Campbell, Miss Marguerite	Bolton	
Chapman, Mrs Agnes	Danby	
Coates, Mrs. Helen	Constable Burton and Northallerton	,,
Dixon, Mrs. Helena	Northallerton	,,
Dunn, Miss Jane	Constable Burton ,, ...	
Farmer, Miss Fanny	Northallerton	
Firby, Miss Mary	Danby	
Fowler, Mrs.	Bolton	,,
Fox, Miss Gertrude	Constable Burton and Northallerton	
Hobson, Mrs. Phylis	,, ,, ,, ,, ...	Whole & part
Lambert, Miss May	Constable Burton	Part time
Lawson, Miss Ethel	,, ,, ...	,,
Peacock, Mrs. Agnes	Bolton and Northallerton	,,
Pearson, Miss Margaret	Constable Burton...	,,
Riddell, Mrs. Edith	Constable Burton and Northallerton	
Scrope, Mrs. Mercedes	Danby	Whole time
Storey, Miss Madge	Bedale	Part time
Sharples, Miss Muriel	Bolton, Constable Burton, Northallerton ...	Part time
Wilkinson, Miss Hilda	Military Hospital, Catterick	Whole time
Wyvill, Mrs. Elizabeth	Constable Burton and Northallerton	Part time

Nurses in the newly prepared billiard room awaiting soldiers' arrival

59

This Certificate is presented by the Army Council, as a permanent record of their thanks, to be placed in the building which has been known and used as

The Bolton Dale Hospital

for British sick and wounded during the Great War, 1914-1919.

Winston S. Churchill

The War Office,
London,
July, 1920.

This letter from Winston Churchill was on the back of the scroll presented to the hospital at the end of the war.

The Yorks./17 Men's VAD Detachment and Yorks./16 Women's VAD Detachment attended regular training camps to prepare themselves for service. Here they are pictured at one such camp in the Dales.

Will Pickles of Aysgarth

Dr William Norman Pickles was born in Leeds in 1885. His father was a general practitioner and Will and four of his five brothers followed him into studying medicine and becoming general practitioners too. There was some financial hardship in the family while they were all studying so Will dispensed medicines for a general practitioner in the evenings earning tea and fifteen shillings a week. He often had to finish surgeries for his employer when he was called out on a case and

so developed knowledge and skills that were to prove useful to him in his own future career.

Dr. Pickles performed several locum duties at Bedale, doing his rounds by bicycle. He also acted as locum at Aysgarth Practice eventually buying into a partnership there in 1913 with Dr Dunbar who had been a fellow medical student with him. The practice served eight villages and the district had a population of 4267 people.

Photo shows Dr Pickles with local VAD nurses, probably when they were doing some training. It is possible that they are Yorks 16 Detachment members. WW1 broke out the following year and Dr Pickles joined the Royal Navy serving in the Atlantic, where he studied the health problems of sailors and first developed his life-long interest in epidemiology. In 1917 he married Gertrude Adelaide Tunstill, the daughter of a wealthy mill owner from Burnley. They had a daughter, Patience and lived initially in Dover while Will finished his naval work. After the war had ended the family moved back to Aysgarth where Gertie helped Will with the running of the practice.

Dr. Pickles practised at Aysgarth for 53 years where apart from caring for the families in his area he carried out research into such subjects as catarrhal jaundice, epidemic myalgia, measles and farmer's lung. He described this work in his book "Epidemiology in a Country Practice" which became a classic book in the medical profession. He travelled all over the world delivering lectures on his work and was awarded numerous awards including a CBE. He was the first President of the Royal College of General Practitioners which was a great honour.

He died in 1969 of pneumonia at the age of 83 and his obituary in the British Medical Journal describes him as " probably the most distinguished country doctor of our time." He was well known in Wensleydale for being careful in his recording and visiting, never underrating a patient or his symptoms, being courteous and kind to all.

These personal characteristics were voiced in a poem by a local lady, Joan Pomfret which is recorded in John Pemberton's biography of Dr Pickles.

> Wind shakes the trees, year in year out,
> Full blown, December bare:
> He knows each face and cottage door,
> Each hearth and narrow stair;
> The rain's song and the river's song
> The living and the dead
> And all the troubles and the pains,
> He cured and comforted.
>
> Early and late, the seasons through,
> This was the path he chose,
> A country doctor on his rounds....
> And everybody knows
> His voice, his smile, the way he walks,
> His presence in the vale,
> They will remember evermore
> His name in Wensleydale.

Madge Blades – VAD Nurse and Aysgarth Practice Dispenser

Madge Blades was born at Mill Farm in 1890 and was the dispenser to the Aysgarth Practice for more than 40 years.

During WW1 she nursed as a VAD in a Leeds hospital and wanted to continue nursing as a career after the war had ended but like so many of her VAD contemporaries she was forced to return to Aysgarth for family reasons. Dr Pickles helped her to lead the useful and practical life she craved by training her to dispense medicines, understanding the type of remedies she was handing out and their measurement. She became an expert in putting the pleat in the white paper wrapping round the bottle and applying the sealing wax neatly.

She went on to perform other tasks such as maintaining the panel cards, mastering the telephone exchange, calling through to the hospital in Northallerton or ambulance on behalf of the locum doctors, keeping the accounts and collecting unpaid fees. The latter task involved her walking or taking a bus up and down the dale as she never mastered the art of riding a bicycle.

Like Dr Pickles she acquired a vast knowledge of all the families in the dale and was much appreciated by them.

Crathorne Hall Red Cross Hospital

The montage above was composed by Miss Pearl Crake from photographs she took while staying at the Hall in 1915. The convalescing soldiers are shown involved in various recreational activities near the stable block, while Sergeant Newman knits a string vest for the boys at the Front – an early example of occupational therapy.

The Commanding Officer, Mrs Dugdale, is seen in the centre of the montage and seated in the centre of the bottom right photograph is her husband Lionel Dugdale. The Rector of All Saints', Crathorne, is pictured in the bottom left hand photograph. These two pictures were taken outside the gardeners' cottages at the Hall.

Mr and Mrs Dugdale opened Crathorne Hall as a Voluntary Aid Detachment Hospital in November 1914 with Belgian soldiers, and subsequently British wounded, being quartered in the cottages and stable block following their initial treatment in Newcastle. The soldiers wore a distinctive uniform of light blue with red ties. They were cared for

18

"Crathorne Hall Hospital," Yarm-on-Tees.

Building lent by	...	J. Lionel Dugdale, Esq.
Date of opening	...	November 13th, 1914.
Date of closing	...	July 9th, 1917.
No. of Beds...	...	24.
Total number of patients treated	...	423.
No. of deaths	...	None.
Hospital affiliated to	...	War Hospital, Newcastle-on-Tyne.
Commandant	...	Mrs. J. Lionel Dugdale, O.B.E.
Medical Officer		Alexander H. Smith, Esq., M.B., C.M.
Secretary ...	...	Miss Lilian Key.
Staffed by ...	Yorks./24 and Trained Nurses and Masseuse.

This Hospital was organised and maintained by Mr. & Mrs. Lionel Dugdale entirely at their own expense. For nearly three years much valuable work was done.

by the VAD (24th Yorks) of the British Red Cross, commanded by Mrs Maud Violet Dugdale. She is remembered as a most dedicated and successful nurse, and in later years would don her uniform to attend the sick in the village.

The medical officer, Dr. Alexander Smith gave his service free but the mileage of his car was paid for by Mr Dugdale as he lived some distance away.

A group of soldiers playing bowls near the stable block, watched by the Rev W A Felton.

A World War I biplane on a field at Five Houses. Such visits by the airmen were frequent, but appear to have been social events without any military significance!

Empire Day 1916

During the difficult days of 1916 when casualties were mounting on the Western Front, Empire Day was celebrated in Crathorne with patriotic fervour. The entry in the Rector's Diary for May 19th describes the day:

"Mr and Mrs Lionel Dugdale of Crathorne Hall were the promoters of the Empire Day celebration and the donors of the numerous and handsome prizes consisting of silver cups, silver models of the Coronation Chair in Westminster Abbey, and silver medals. The prizes were for the best essays on the British Empire written by children attending the Day Schools of Crathorne, Hilton, Hutton Rudby, Kirk Levington, Worsall and Yarm. At 2.45 pm the children of the various schools assembled near the Rectory and marched in procession to Crathorne Hall. First came a highly decorated lurry (sic) driven by Mr Towers, farm bailiff, on which were a pianist, a cornet player, and a drummer. Miss Beryl Dugdale as Britannia, Miss Margaret Randolph as Peace and several boys and girls representing the United Kingdom, our Colonies and dependencies came next, followed by all the children carrying flags. On arrival at the Hall the children saluted the Union Jack, and were addressed by the Rector of Yarm on "Citizenship". Then followed a splendid tea provided by Mr and Mrs Dugdale. After tea the prizes were distributed and Mrs Dugdale addressed the children on their responsibility as citizens of the great British Empire".

The event was one of many organised by Mr and Mrs Dugdale. These included the annual Christmas dinner and dance at the Hall as well as the Christmas tea party for the children. We read that "joints of beef were presented to every resident. Cardigans and other presents were distributed by Mrs Dugdale." (Crathorne Village Record).

The girls from left to right: Renee Towers (Scotland), ?? (Wales), Margaret Randolph (Peace), Beryl Dugdale (Britannia), Evelyn Culling (England), Lucy Culling (Ireland). The boys have not been identified.

Lionel Dugdale standing, in characteristic pose, leaning on his stick. His wife, Violet, is beside him. They and the Crathorne contingent are outside the Reading Room ready to march to the Hall.

Numerous events took place in the Reading Room including one at the beginning of the war which was reported as follows: "At a meeting of the men employed on the Crathorne estate, it was unanimously agreed that every man should give a weekly voluntary contribution to the Prince of Wales' National Relief Fun (The Northern Star, 15th August, 1914). The significant sum of between £4.00 and £6.00 was sent regularly to the fund.

Yorks./24. Crathorne and Yarm.

Commandant : Mrs. J. Lionel Dugdale, O.B.E.

Name.	Record of War Service.	Part time or Whole time.
Dugdale, Mrs. Maud Violet	Commandant. Crathorne Hall Hospital	Whole time
Burnupp, Mrs. Elizabeth	Quartermaster. ,, ,,	Part time
Archer, Mrs. Margaret	Surgical Nurse. ,, ,,	,,
Richardson, Miss Constance	,, ,,	,,
Dickenson, Mrs. Margaret	,, ,,	,,
Fawcett, Miss Mary	,, ,,	,,
Scarbrough, Mrs. Emily	,, ,,	,,
Stuart, Miss Margaret	,, ,,	,,
Welford, Miss Martha	,, ,,	,,
Hanham. Miss Frances	,, ,,	,,
Mars, Miss Elizabeth	,, ,,	,,
Swales, Mrs. Martha	,, ,,	,,
Snushall, Miss Elizabeth	,, ,,	,,
Ward, Mrs. Cicely	,, ,,	,,
Bolton, Mrs. Edith	,, ,,	,,
Snowdon, Mrs. Annie	,, ,,	,,
Fawcett, Mrs. Adeline	,, ,,	,,
Watson, Miss Evelyn	Crathorne Hall Hospital and Eaglescliffe V.A.D. Hospital	,,
Watson, Miss Mabel	V.A.D. Hospital, Middleton St. George	,,
Harrison, Miss Edith	V.A.D. Hospital, Middleton St. George	,,
Harrison, Miss Gladys	Crathorne Hall Hospital	,,

Cober Hill Hospital

Cober Hill belonged to Lord Airedale (Baron Airedale of Gledhow) formerly known as Albert Kitson, a Leeds industrialist. It was a splendid Victorian mansion and in 1920 was purchased by Arnold Rowntree of the Quaker and chocolate family and converted into a residential centre and conference venue for people working in education, social services and other charitable voluntary activities. During the war, Arnold Rowntree as MP for York, championed the cause of Quakers who were conscientious objectors but were needing opportunities for service. This eventually resulted in the establishment of the Friends' Ambulance Unit.

Today Cober Hill is a hotel providing conference and residential facilities.

Yorks ./ 15 Men's VAD Cloughton Detachment had 44 men in 1914. Their commandant and medical officer was Dr. Bernard Gilpin Forman, a local GP. In 1918 the Red Cross North Riding Branch WW1 Report states:

"The Detachment met weekly at the beginning of the year and revised all their knowledge including first aid, sanitation and hygiene. They drilled every week for three months and were to have resumed weekly drills in October 1917 but owing to the Commandant's professional work increasing he was unable to undertake them longer.

Every night during the week one of the Detachment acts as night orderly at Cober Hill Hospital and during this duty they have had to do small dressings, feed any patients requiring it and take temperatures. These duties are all recorded in a book for the medical officer to see in the morning. They also during night duty sweep and scrub out the dry room and lower corridor of the hospital, light the kitchen fire, clean out the flues and fill lamps. One of their principle duties at night has been to see that all lights were shaded and I think only three times during the past year the coast patrol complained about lights which speaks highly of the orderlies' work.

Many of them have had to come a considerable distance in all weathers to duty.

They have all helped during the year in the transport of the various convoys received for the hospital at the station.

If the men of the Detachment had not done night duty, it would have meant another nurse if not two nurses."

"Cober Hill Hospital," Cloughton, Scarborough.

Building lent by	... ...	The Lord Airedale.
Date of opening	... ...	25th November, 1914.
Date of closing	... ...	7th March, 1919.
No. of Beds ...	... ...	... 35.
Total number of patients treated	... ...	716.
No. of deaths	... ...	None.
Hospital affiliated to	...	Military Hospital, York.
Commandant	...	B. G. Forman, Esq., M.D., M.B.E.
Medical Officers	...	B. G. Forman, Esq., M.D., M.B.E.
		Frank Godfrey, Esq., M.D.
Matron	...	Miss Alice McNabb, A.R.R.C. (Honorary).
Staffed by	... ...	Yorks./15 and 22.

Soldiers at Cober Hill with the staff and a dog.

Yorks./22. Scarbrough.

Commandant : Miss A. Tindall.

Medical Officer : Dr. R. Cuff.

Name.	Record of War Service.	Part time or Whole time
Tindall, Miss Augusta	Vice-President and Commandant, raised large sums of money, supplied V.A.D.'s for Hospitals at home and abroad, etc.	
Appleyard, Miss Rachael	Sea Bathing, Scarbrough, etc.	Part time
Appleyard, Miss Sara	,, ,, ,,	,,
Athy, Miss Eleanor	Military Hospital, Bradford, and others	Whole time
Baker, Miss Elizabeth	Sea Bathing, Scarbrough	Part time
Blakey, Miss Mary	Cober Hill V. A. D. Hospital	Whole time
Dawson, Miss Ida	Royal Chelsea Military Hospital	,,
Eyre, Mrs. Christine	Sea Bathing Hospital, Scarbrough	Part time
McNab, Miss Alice	4 years at Cober Hill as Matron	,,
Maw, Miss Laura	4½ years at Cober Hill	Whole time
Maw, Miss Jenny	Cook, still in France	,,
Parker, Mrs. Louise	Cober Hill and Sea Bathing, Scarbrough	Part time
Pritchard, Miss Amy	2nd Western Military Hospital	Whole time
Pegge, Miss Elizabeth T.	Still in France	,,
Sawer, Miss Hilda	Sea Bathing, Scarbrough, etc.	Part time
Walters, Miss Jeanette	Cober Hill	,,
Woodhouse, Miss Lilian	No. 17 V. A. D. Hospital, Durham	4 years
Williamson, Miss Violette	Belper, Perth Hospitals and others	Whole time
Vickerman, Miss Nora	St. George's Hospital, Harrogate	,,
Cowton, Miss Alice	Cober Hill	,,
Garbutt, Miss Minnie	Officer's Hospital, Scarbrough	Part time
McKay, Miss Florence	Sea Bathing and Cober Hill	,,
Cain, Miss Agnes	Matron. France	3 years
Cobb, Miss Violet	Officer's Hospital, Scarbrough, till closed	Whole time
Stewart, Miss Beatrice	Scarbrough, Dean Road Hospital	1 year
Masters, Miss Elizabeth	Borough Sanatorium	Whole time
Longstaffe, Miss Harriett	4½ years R. N. S. B. Infirmary, Scarbrough	,,
Heffer, Miss Edith M. L.	2 years Nursing Cober Hill	,,
Botterill, Miss Mabel	Cober Hill and Duffield	Part time
Holmes, Miss Kate	S. B. Infirmary	,,
Griffin, Mrs. Evelyn	Cober Hill	,,
Lance, Miss Doreen	Queen Margaret's Officers' Hospital	,,
Smith, Miss Olive	Cober Hill	,,
Walker, Miss Mary E.	Cober Hill	Whole time
Harland, Mrs. Lily	Masham Hospital	,,
Jaconides, Mrs. Lydia	Quartermaster. St. Dunstan's	,,
Abraham, Miss Kathleen	2nd Western General Hospital till closed	,,
Abraham, Miss Nora	,, ,, ,,	,,
Christian, Miss Marjory	Officers' Hospital, Oakham, and Ripon Camp	,,
Pain, Miss Lizzie	Officers' Hospital, Oakham till closed	,,
Abelitt, Miss Kathleen	Officers' Hospital, Oakham	,,

Constable Burton Red Cross Hospital

19
"The Red Cross Hospital," Constable Burton.

Building lent by	...	the late M. D'arcy Wyvill, Esq.
Date of opening	...	October 16th, 1914.
Date of closing	...	December, 1915.
No. of Beds ...	...	... 12.
No. of deaths	...	None.
Commandant	...	Mrs. D'arcy Wyvill.
Medical Officer	...	Dr. Jas. Peacock, Leyburn.
Matron ...	...	Mrs. Hobson (Honorary).
Staffed by ...	...	Yorks./16.

This Hospital was organised, equipped and maintained entirely by Mrs. D'arcy Wyvill and treated Belgian soldiers during the early days of the War, and latterly convalescent soldiers.

This hospital was located in Constable Burton Hall which is 3 miles east of Leyburn. The name of Constable Burton is believed to have come about from the 12th Century when a man called Roald was given the lordship of the manor of Burton as part of his wages for being Constable or Keeper of Richmond Castle. So it became Constable's Burton.

The house was designed by John Carr of York and dates from 1768 though it was built on an earlier Elizabethan structure. More recently, it featured in an episode in the British TV series "All Creatures Great and Small"

One of the earlier members of the Wyvill family, Marmaduke Wyvill, was Liberal MP for Richmond between 1847 and 1868 and had two further claims to fame. One was that he was the runner up in the first International Chess Tournament in 1851 and the other was that he proposed to Florence Nightingale and was rejected.

His son Marmaduke D'Arcy Wyvill was the Liberal MP for Otley from 1895 to 1900 and it was he who offered the house as a hospital in WW1. He was elected by the British Red Cross Society nationally to serve on the War Committee but died in 1918.

The house is still owned by the Wyvill family today.

Mrs D'Arcy Wyvill is shown at the foot of the steps outside Constable Burton Hall. The nurse 2 rows behind her is Laura Horsley whose father was the station master at Leyburn.

Yorks./16. Constable Burton.

Commandant : Mrs. D'arcy Wyvill.

Medical Officer : Dr. Jas. Peacock.

Name.	Record of War Service.	Part time or Whole time.
Barclay, Lady Letitia ...	Bolton and Northallerton Hospitals	Part time
Beswick, Miss Maud ...	Northallerton	,,
Bosvile, Miss Helen ...	Bolton and Northallerton	,,
Bowes, Miss Helena ...	Bolton and Northallerton	,,
Broadley, Miss Margaret ...	Northallerton	
Campbell, Miss Marguerite ...	Bolton	
Chapman, Mrs Agnes ...	Danby	,,
Coates, Mrs. Helen ...	Constable Burton and Northallerton	,,
Dixon, Mrs. Helena ...	Northallerton	
Dunn, Miss Jane ...	Constable Burton	
Farmer, Miss Fanny ...	Northallerton	
Firby, Miss Mary ...	Danby	,,
Fowler, Mrs. ...	Bolton	,,
Fox, Miss Gertrude ...	Constable Burton and Northallerton	
Hobson, Mrs. Phylis ...	,, ,, ,, ,, ...	Whole & part
Lambert, Miss May ..	Constable Burton	Part time
Lawson, Miss Ethel ..	,, ,, ...	,,
Peacock, Mrs. Agnes ...	Bolton and Northallerton	,,
Pearson, Miss Margaret ..	Constable Burton...	,,
Riddell, Mrs. Edith ...	Constable Burton and Northallerton	
Scrope, Mrs. Mercedes ..	Danby	Whole time
Storey, Miss Madge ..	Bedale	Part time
Sharples, Miss Muriel ..	Bolton, Constable Burton, Northallerton	Part time
Wilkinson, Miss Hilda ...	Military Hospital, Catterick	Whole time
Wyvill, Mrs. Elizabeth ...	Constable Burton and Northallerton	Part time

Of the V.A.Ds listed above Gertrude Fox was the cook at the house and Miss Muriel Sharples became companion to Edith Wyvill. Mrs Helen Coates's husband was the coachman, and Miss May Lambert had previously been a school mistress. Mrs Elizabeth Wyvill was the step grandmother to the current owner of Constable Burton Hall, Mr Charles Wyvill.

The North Riding Red Cross financial report records for 1914 state that it cost £15 to maintain 10 men for 3 weeks, £3 to maintain 6 men for 1 week and £14 to maintain 4 men for 7 weeks.

The hospital was organised, equipped and maintained entirely by Mrs. D'Arcy Wyvill

Danby Hall Hospital

"Danby Hall Hospital," Middleham.

Building lent by		Hy. Scrope, Esq.
Date of opening		16th October, 1914.
Date of closing		... July, 1915.
No. of Beds		... 10.
Total number of patients treated		... 10.
No. of deaths		None.
Commandant		Mrs. Henry Scrope.
Medical Officer ...		Dr. Geo. Cockcroft, Middleham.
Staffed by		Private Staff and Trained Nurse.

This hospital was established, organised and maintained entirely by Mr. and Mrs. Henry Scrope and treated Belgian soldiers in the early days of the war.

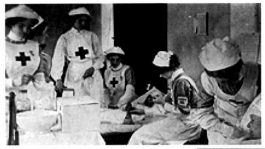

Members of Yorks./16 VAD nurses practising their nursing skills at Danby Hall.

Yorks./16. Constable Burton.

Commandant : Mrs. D'arcy Wyvill
Medical Officer : Dr. Jas. Peacock.

Name.	Record of War Service.	Part time or Whole time.
Barclay, Lady Letitia	Bolton and Northallerton Hospitals	Part time
Beswick, Miss Maud	Northallerton	
Bosvile, Miss Helen	Bolton and Northallerton	
Bowes, Miss Helena	Bolton and Northallerton	
Broadley, Miss Margaret	Northallerton	
Campbell, Miss Marguerite	Bolton	
Chapman, Mrs Agnes	Danby	
Coates, Mrs. Helen	Constable Burton and Northallerton	
Dixon, Mrs. Helena	Northallerton	
Dunn, Miss Jane	Constable Burton	
Farmer, Miss Fanny	Northallerton	
Firby, Miss Mary	Danby	
Fowler, Mrs.	Bolton	
Fox, Miss Gertrude	Constable Burton and Northallerton	
Hobson, Mrs. Phylis	„ „ „ „	Whole & part
Lambert, Miss May	Constable Burton	Part time
Lawson, Miss Ethel	„ „	
Peacock, Mrs. Agnes	Bolton and Northallerton	
Pearson, Miss Margaret	Constable Burton...	
Riddell, Mrs. Edith	Constable Burton and Northallerton	
Scrope, Mrs. Mercedes	Danby	Whole time
Storey, Miss Madge	Bedale	Part time
Sharples, Miss Muriel	Bolton, Constable Burton, Northallerton	Part time
Wilkinson, Miss Hilda	Military Hospital, Catterick	Whole time
Wyvill, Mrs. Elizabeth	Constable Burton and Northallerton	Part time

Duncombe Park Hospital

"Duncombe Park Hospital," Helmsley.

Building lent by	...	The late Earl of Feversham.	
Date of opening	...	...	June 28th, 1915.
Date of closing	...	...	January 24th, 1919.
No. of Beds ...	...	...	50.
Total number of patients treated	...	...	650.
No. of deaths	...	...	None.
Hospital affiliated to	...	... Military Hospital, York.	
Commandants	...	The Lady Marjorie Beckett.	
		Mrs. Harrison Holt.	
		Mrs. E. Shaw, O.B.E.	
Medical Officers	...	... A. C. Blair, Esq., M.D.	
		T. Walsh-Tetley, Esq., M.R.C.S.	
Secretary ...	...	... E. Creighton, Esq.	
Staffed by Yorks./78.	Helmsley.	Yorks./40. Kirbymoorside.	
Yorks./72.	Kirkdale.		

Duncombe Park is set in 300 acres of parkland near to Helmsley in the North York Moors National Park. The house was built in 1713 by a Yorkshire gentleman architect William Wakefield who received advice from Sir John Vanbrugh, responsible for designing Castle Howard nearby.

In 1915 the house was offered as a hospital by the 2nd Earl of Feversham whose grandfather the 1st Earl had died that year in January. The 2nd Earl was a politician and soldier who died on September 15th, 1916 in the Battle of the Somme. He was buried there with his deerhound who died with him in the battle.

His widow, Lady Marjorie Blanche Eva Greville, a daughter of the Earl of Warwick became the Commandant of the hospital for the duration of the war.

Yorks./40. Kirbymoorside.

Commandant: Mrs. Holt.

Medical Officer: Dr. T. W. Tetley.

Name.	Record of War Service.	Part time or Whole time.
Holt, Mrs. Adolpha Wykeham	Commandant. Duncombe Park Hospital	Part time
Burnett, Mrs. Janet	Superintendent. ,, ,,	,,
Benton, Miss Charlotte	Quartermaster. ,, ,,	,,
Tetley, Dr. T. Walsh	,, ,,	,,
Beck, Miss Maud	,, ,,	,,
Bowes, Miss Gladys	,, ,,	,,
Carter, Miss Frances	2 years Military Hospital, Catterick Camp	Whole time
Cole, Miss Muriel	Duncombe Park Hospital	Part time
Conning, Miss Margaret	,, ,,	,,
Hill, Mrs. Henrietta	,, ,,	,,
Hill, Mrs. Mary A.	,, ,,	,,
Hill, Miss Anne	,, ,,	,,
Holt, Miss Evelyn A.	3 years London Gen. Hosps and 25th Stationary Hosp. France	Whole time
Holt, Miss Dorothy	Duncombe Park Hospital	Part time
Jackson, Miss Grace	,, ,,	,,
Jackson, Miss Nancy	,, ,,	,,
Kay, Miss Anne	,, ,,	,,
Mattory, Miss Helen	,, ,,	,,
Odell, Miss Clara	,, ,,	,,
Potter, Miss Mary I.	2 years Military Hospital, Catterick Camp	Whole time
Richardson, Miss Anne	Duncombe Park Hopdital	Part time
Richardson, Miss Blanche	,, ,,	,,
Richardson, Miss Elsie	,, ,,	,,
Shepherd, Miss Susan	,, ,,	,,
Shepherd, Miss Mary S.	,, ,,	,,
Walker, Miss Lucy	,, ,,	,,
Watson, Mrs. Mabel	,, ,,	,,
Wilkinson, Miss Edith	,, ,,	,,
White, Miss Frances	,, ,,	,,
Calam, Miss Maud	,, ,,	,,
Benton, Miss Janet	,, ,,	,,
Elliott, Miss M. A.	,, ,,	,,
Richardson, Miss Dora	,, ,,	,,

VAD Nurses at Duncombe Park. Lady Marjorie Duncombe is standing second from left wearing the badge of the 21st KRR Yeoman Rifles.

A group of convalescing patients, VAD nurses and visitors outside Duncombe Park. Was this a soldier marrying his sweetheart at the hospital?

Nurses of 40th Yorks VAD pose at Kirbymoorside during the First World War.

Yorks./72. Kirkdale.

Commandant : Mrs. Edward Shaw, O.B.E.
Medical Officer : Dr. J. F. Porter, O.B.E.

Name.	Record of War Service.	Part time or Whole time.
Shaw, Mrs. Edward, O.B.E.	Duncombe Park and Welburn Hall Hospitals	Whole time
Powell, Mrs. Lilian	Quartermaster	Part time
Porter, Dr. J. Francis	"	"
Aydon, Mrs. Alice	"	"
Barker, Miss Edith	Welburn Hall Hospital	"
Barker, Miss Ethel	Duncombe Park and Welburn Hall Hospital	"
Barker, Mrs. Louie	Welburn Hall Hospital	"
Bell, Miss Annie	Duncombe Park and Welburn Hall Hospital	"
Bray, Mrs. Lily	" " "	"
Brown, Miss Evelyn	" " "	"
Bucktin, Miss Francis E.	Welburn Hall Hospital	"
Cadman, Miss Eveline	Duncombe Park and Welburn Hall Hospital	"
Carpenter, Miss Alice	" " "	"
Colley, Miss Hannah J.	" " "	"
Dixon, Miss Constance	" " "	"
Dodds, Miss Annie	" " "	"
Ford, Miss Christiana	Welburn Hall Hospital	"
Hall, Miss Amy	Welburn Hall Hospital	"
Hill, Miss Esther	Duncombe Park and Welburn Hall Hospital	"
Hornby, Miss Mary	" " "	"
Huffington, Mrs. Kate	" " "	"
Marwood, Mrs. Harriet	" " "	"
Peacock, Miss Margery	" " "	"
Read, Miss Mary	" " "	"
Robinson, Miss Caroline	" " "	"
Sunley, Mrs. Jane	" " "	"
Stokell, Mrs. Jane	" " "	"
Swales, Miss Elsie	" " "	"
Slater, Mrs. Louisa	" " "	"
Warriner, Mrs. Eleanor	Welburn Hall Hospital	"
Warriner, Miss Frances	Welburn Hall Hospital	"
Wass, Miss Ellis	Duncombe Park and Welburn Hall Hospital	"
Winnall, Mrs. Ada	Welburn Hall Hospital	"
White, Mrs. Julia	Duncombe Park and Welburn Hall Hospital	"
Wood, Miss Maggie	" " "	"

The hospital produced half yearly reports and below is a copy covering the period January 1st to June 30th 1916.

DUNCOMBE PARK HOSPITAL.

Half Yearly Report, Jan. 1st to June 30th, 1916

The Duncombe Park Hospital has now been open for one year, and this is the second half-yearly report. It has treated 88 patients during this period.

Since the publication of the last Report, two extra beds have been added, making a total now of 22 beds. Also two open-air huts have been put on the terraces for the cases who need fresh air treatment.

A permanent and fully qualified Masseuse has been added to the Staff, and the patients have greatly benefitted by her treatment, so much so indeed, that a great many cases are saved from partial disablement in after life by this means, therefore the Committee think that when this is fully realized, it will be understood that though an expensive addition, this is a very necessary one.

The painting and distempering of the Hospital has been an additional extra expense, and also the renewal of chairs and linoleum in the recreation room and some of the wards.

EXECUTIVE COMMITTEE: The Countess of Feversham (Chairman), Mrs Duncombe, Mrs E. Shaw, Mrs Holt, Mrs Fuller, The Rev. H. E. Newton (Chairman of Finance Committee), Mr E. H. A. Cooper (Hon. Treasurer), Mrs Peter, Mr E. Creighton (Hon. Secretary and Senior Orderly).

FINANCE COMMITTEE: The Rev. H. E. Newton (Chairman) Mr E. Creighton (Hon. Secretary), Mr James Peter, Col. C. W. E. Duncombe, Mr E. H. A. Cooper (Hon. Treasurer).

COMMITTEE OF ORDERLIES: Mr Ernest Creighton (Senior Orderly), Rev. H. E. Newton (Vicar of Helmsley), Rev. F. W. Ramsden, Rev. J. W. G. Bennett, Messrs E. H. A. Cooper, C. E. Buckley, W. Armstrong, B. Frank, J. Frank, E. Williams, A. Spence, W. H. F. Hoodless, G. F. Fletcher, Jas. Peter, Wadsworth, J. C. Frank, Jr., H. W. Plows.

HON. TREASURER: Mr. E. H. A. Cooper, Barclay's Bank, Helmsley.

HON. SECRETARY: Mr. Ernest Creighton, Beckett's Bank, Helmsley.

MEDICAL OFFICERS: A. C. Blair, M.D., J. F. Porter, M.D. T. W. Tetley, M.R.C.S.

DETACHMENTS.

(1) KIRBYMOORSIDE. (Yorkshire 40).

Medical Officer : Dr. Tetley. Commandant : Mrs. Holt.
Lady Superintendent : Mrs. Burnett.
Quartermaster : Miss Benton.

V.A.D. NURSES : Miss Odell, Miss S. Shepherd, Miss Kay,
Miss Holt, Miss D. Holt, Miss Richardson, Miss Elliott, Miss
B. Richardson, Mrs Ernest Hill, Miss Lucy Walker, Miss Grace
Jackson, Mrs. Herbert Jackson, Mrs. Glover, Miss Carter, Miss
Calam, Miss Nancy Jackson, Miss Cole, Mrs. J. Hill, Miss
Wilkinson, Miss Holliday, Mrs. Scaling, Miss Potter, Miss D.
Richardson.

(2) KIRKDALE, (Yorkshire 72)

Medical Officer : Dr. Porter. Commandant : Mrs. Edward Shaw
Quartermaster : Mrs. Powell.

V.A.D. NURSES : Mrs. Alice Aydon, Miss Ethel Barker, Miss
Evelyn Brown, Miss Kate Emmett, Miss M Hornby, Miss
Esther Hill, Miss Mary Read Miss Caroline Robinson, Mrs.
Louisa Slater, Mrs. Jane Stokell, Mrs Jane Sunley, Miss Annie
Bell, Miss M. Wood, Miss Carpenter, Miss Swales, Miss Dodds
Miss Bumby, Mrs Bray.

(3) HELMSLEY, (Yorkshire 78).

Medical Officer : Dr. Blair. Commandant : The Countess
of Feversham. Quartermaster : Mrs. Porter.
Secretary : Miss D. Duckworth.

V.A.D. WORKERS : Mrs. Hawkins, Miss H. Sunley, Miss F.
Sample, Miss I. Richardson, Miss O Pickard Miss L. Palmer,
Miss Ethel King, Miss A. Keen, Miss L. Kirby, Miss G Haw-
kins, Miss G. Garbutt, Miss S. Garbutt, Mrs. Palmer, Miss
Dennis, Mrs. Dale, Miss Bloodworth, Mrs Blair, Miss H
Barker, Miss K. M. Baldwin, Mrs Allenby, Miss Logan Miss
Hutchinson, Miss Waines, Miss J. Temple Mrs. Reggie
Atkinson, Miss B. Dale, Miss Marsden, Miss McNeill.

Lady Feversham and members of the Helmsley Detachment
wish particularly to thank Sergeant Jackson for taking the
weekly Stretcher Drill.

TRAINED NURSES.

Nurse M. A Burch was appointed Sister-in-Charge of the
Hospital in January, and has proved herself most excellent and
efficient in this capacity.

MASSEUSE. Miss Mathilde Bengtsson, Medical Gymnast,
Diploma of the Royal Institute of Medical Gymnastics and
Massage, Stockholm, from the Belgian Hospital at Virval,
Calais, came to work at the Hospital on May 22nd.

The lists of patients from the report, reproduced on the following page, demonstrate the wide variation of conditions that the soldiers suffered from, the length of time their treatment took and the number of different regiments they represented.

80

Admitted	No	Name	Regiment	Nature of Disability	Discharged
Nov 5th	10398	Pte C Knott	8th Devonshire	Rheumatic Fever	Jan 14th
Nov 5th	8755	Pte R Asdale	Depot West Yorks	Gun Shot Chest	Mar 10th
Nov 6th	14659	Pte J Ellicott	8th Devonshire	Rheumatic Fever	Jan 14th
Nov 6th	36357	Dvr S Smith	R. F. A.	Rheumatic Fever	Feb 12th
Nov 5th	411	Pte A T Poole	1st WelshGuards	Gun Shot right foot	Feb 3rd
Nov 5th	10490	Pte A Hancock	9th Lancers	Colitis	Feb 9th
Nov 5th	12044	Lce Cprl G Fala	6th Cameron Hdrs	Bronchitis	Feb 12th
Nov 5th	2929	., J W Baker	6th South Staffs	V. D. H.	Feb 12th
Nov 5th	2966	Rfm D W Hum	18th London	Contusion, knee	Feb 12th
Nov 5th	15297	Sgt P J Charlton	8th K. O. S. B.	Gunshot, left foot	June 22nd
Nov 5th	2213	Cpl P F Salmon	Royal Horse Guards	Fracture left fibula	Mar 4th
Nov 5th	21994	Pte H Atkinson	2nd Worcestershire	Sciatica	Feb 9th
Nov 5th	4081	Gnr G W Brett	R. H. A.	Fracture left foot	Feb 14th
Dec 21st	2984	Pte J Collier	5th Yorks	Gunshot left foot	Mar 11th
Feb 4th	094997	Pte J Broughton	A. S. C.	Nephritis	Feb 24th
Feb 4th	17283	Pte C Warne	9th West Yorks	Lumbar sprain	Mar 4th
Feb 4th	19171	Pte E Beedle	3rd West Yorks	Valvular Disease of Heart	Mar 4th
Feb 4th	28810	Pte A Webster	1st Liverpool	Rheumatic Fever	Mar 4th
Feb 4th	12268	Pte S Steward	4th West Yorks	Neurasthenia	Mar 4th
Feb 4th	13891	Pte F Green	3rd Dorset	Frostbite feet	April 8th
Feb 4th	12147	Pte F Birkett	4th West Yorks	Bright's Disease & Rheumatic Fever	Mar 4th
Feb 4th	16997	Cpl J W Smith	6th Yorks	Gun Shot left shoulder and chest	Mar 4th
Mar 11th	S/4363	Lc Cpl D S Ford	9th Royal Highlanders	Gun shot wound left shoulder	June 2nd
Mar 11th	6925	Pte A Rainbow	2nd Bedford Reg	Gun shot wound left leg	
Mar 11th	1440	Pte W Budworth	4th Leicester Reg	Gun shot right thigh, amp. right leg	June 26th
Mar 11th	20067	Pte G G Attenboro'	5th Shropshire L. I.	Gun shot, Compound frac. left tibia	June 10th
Mar 11th	4822	Sgt A Baggeley	A. P. C.	Abscess in right groin	June 6th
June 14th	,,	,,	,,	,,	July 8th

Admitted	No	Name	Regiment	Nature of Disability	Discharged
Mar 11th	6180	Pte S Bethel	Depot East Yorks	Old fracture, necrosis right tibia	June 2nd
Mar 11th	13757	Pte J Nevins	3rd Dorset Reg	Frostbite both feet	June 2nd
Mar 11th	15059	Lc Cpl A Davison	5th Reserve Ca Regt	Pneumonia	May 8th
Mar 11th	8198	Pte H Pearson	4th West York	Pneumonia	June 2nd
April 13th	3381	Pte J Ward	5th Yorks	Gun shot wound chest	June 2nd
April 14th	10985	Lc Cpl A Douce	1st Cameron Hilanders	Rheumatic Fever	June 22nd
April 15th	17907	Pte W H Spinks	A. S. C.	Gun shot wound right hand	June 10th
April 19th	12520	Pte H Pryor	6th York & La	Gun shot wound right middle finger	July 27th
April 15th	514	Sgt W Banks	3rd Northumberland Fusiliers	Rheumatic Fever	June 23rd
April 15th	20872	Pte W Wood	2nd Yorks L. I	Nephritis	May 15th
April 15th	19109	Pte F Robson	9th York & La	Loose cartilage left knee joint	June 23rd
April 15th	15712	Pte R Mc Murray	7th Cameron Highlanders	Gun shot wound right thigh	June 22nd
April 15th	15829	Pte R Burns	1st Royal Scots usiliers	Gun shot wound left chest	June 21st
April 15th	3719	Pte N Osborne	2/5 Northumberland ,,	Pleurisy	June 21st
April 15th	5623	Pte M Baird	5th Reserve Ca Regt	Bronchitis	June 10th
June 14th	8669	Cpl J Wotherspoon	2nd Dragoons	Neurasthenia	
June 14th	19772	Air-Mch G G Motley	Royal Flying Cps	Appendicitis	July 24th
June 14th	17811	Pte J Winstanley	10th Cheshire gt.	Gun shot wound left arm	
June 14th	16239	Pte P Hauton	8th Border Reg	Gun shot wound elbow	
June 14th	15146	Lc Cpl H Roberts	7th Yorks L. I	Gun shot wound chest	
June 14th	12221	Pte E Aspin	2 d East Lanc Regt	Gun shot wound scalp & right leg	
June 14th	31119	Pte H Jones	R. A. M. C	Fracture tibia and fibula	July 17th
June 14th	6904	Pte H Clarke	A Cyclist Cor	Gun shot wound rt. hand & lt. arm	
July 1st	15355	Pte T E Keelan	8th Royal Lan	Gun shot wound left thigh	
July 1st	15787	Pte G Taft	10th Glos. Reg	Gun shot wound rt. arm, leg & thigh	
July 1st	26935	Pte F T Bryan	4th Worcester L.	Gun shot wound left tibia	
July 1st	25068	Dvr A Pink	R. E.	Bronchitis	
July 1st	15/933	Pte N Walker	15th West Yo	Gun shot wound left arm, rt. thigh	
July 1st	3/9430	Pte P Mold	2nd Northam gt	Gun shot wound left calf	
July 1st	9646	Pte T Barnes	1st Royal Ber	Gun shot wound lt. arm, leg & ankle	
July 1st	3573	Pte W Gibbard	15th London	Potts fracture right leg	
July 1st	18841	Air-Mch F Dowling	Royal Flying C	Haematuria	
July 5th	16281	Cpl G Johnson	11th Durham	Gun shot wound right shoulder	

81

One of the questions that the staff asked is why patients who lived in the area could not be transferred to their hospital and the reply from Headquarters can be seen here.

We much regret to hear that Pte. C. Knott, 10398, 8th Devonshire Regiment, who was a patient in this Hospital from November 5th till January 14th, was killed in action in France in June, and that Pte M Baird died after rejoining his regiment

Many letters have been received by the three Commandants from patients who have left the Hospital, expressing their gratitude to the Doctors and Nurses for the kindness and consideration shown to them

Our thanks are due to Miss McNeill for getting up sports for the patients, to Miss Hutchinson for taking night duty for so many consecutive weeks, and to Mr Apse for driving the motor ambulance, and to all those who have contributed in eo many ways to the efficiency of the Hospital, and to the welfare of the men

THE COMMANDANTS' THANKS.

The Commandants wish again to express their grateful thanks to all those who have continued to give their valuable help to the Duncombe Park Hospital, more especially the Medical Officers of the Detachments, Dr. Blair, Dr. Porter, and Dr Tetley, and the members of the three Detachments who have so generously given their services.

The Concerts organised by the Orderlies have been much appreciated by the patients, especially during the long winter evenings; the Commandants feel most grateful to the entertainers for the pleasure they have given to the men

They are also much indebted to Mrs Duncombe and all others for their generous contribution of food, etc.; also to Miss Duckworth for her valuable assistance with the secretarial work.

The Commandants are very sorry that they have not been able to secure more transfers for men whose homes are in the neighbourhood, and for men in the 21st King's Royal Rifle Corps.

The following is an extract from a letter received a fortnight ago from Headquarters on the question of transfers.—

" Owing to the pressure on all Hospitals at the present time, the War Office do not wish transfers to take place from one command to another."

The Commandants hope however, that this regulation will be relaxed shortly, and that the Hospital will be able to benefit the relatives of those living in the district.

(Signed),　　　　　　MARJORIE FEVERSHAM,
　　　　　　　　　　ADELA SHAW,
　　　　　　　　　　A. W. HOLT.

A piece in the local paper of the time says 'Congratulations have been showered on Dr. T. Walsh Tetley of Kirbymoorside, since the presentation to him of a badge of life honorary membership of the British Red Cross Society. Probably there is no man in Yorkshire more worthy of the medallion, Dr. Tetley having been honorary Surgeon to the Kirbymoorside Detachment since its formation as a St. John's Unit in 1911. Dr. Tetley's class of 80 pupils did valuable service during the war, when a hospital was opened in Duncombe Park.

It is interesting to recall that the first Commandant of the Detachment was Mrs. (now Lady) Fuller, who was followed by Mrs. A. W. Hold and the present Commandant, Mrs. J.E.D. Shaw.

Dr. Tetley has just made an urgent appeal for recruits stating that no greater service could be given to the community than by forwarding the work of the Detachment.'

82

The sister of the 2nd Earl of Feversham was Lady D'Abernon who was considered a great beauty with intelligence. She was a charming hostess, supporting her husband's difficult work as the first British Ambassador in Berlin after the war.

During the war she worked for the British Red Cross, nursing in France and Italy and unusually as a qualified anaesthetist. It was her proud boast that she did not lose any of the 1,137 patients to whom she was responsible for administering their anaesthetic!

She published extracts from her diary describing her Red Cross experiences as well as her time at the Embassy in "Red Cross and Berlin Embassy 1915-1926" published in 1946 a copy of which is retained in the British Red Cross Archives Department.

Extracts from her book

"I received unsolicited testimonials of proficiency, not only from Dr Page M.D. but also from Dr Frederick Longhurst M.D. anaesthetist to St Georges Hospital"..." page 144

"During the last 6 months Lady D'Abernon has given a very considerable number of anaesthetics under my supervision. She understands the signs of anaesthesia very well and has a good practical....." p145 in a letter sent from 53 Welbeck Street, London on March 31st 1916.

"I have much pleasure in stating that Lady D'Abernon has administered ether to a large number of patients at St Mark's Hospital, City Road...." P145 letter from 43 Cambridge Street, Hyde Park.

Another remarkable example of the progress of women in accessing different occupations during the war.

Chaloner Hall Hospital

"Chaloner Hall Hospital," Guisbrough.

Building lent by	...	Lord and Lady Gisborough.
Date of opening	...	... 13th December, 1915.
Date of closing	...	... 31st March, 1917.
No. of Beds ...	... ...	... ... 20.
Total number of patients treated	...	... 220.
No. of deaths	...	... ... None.
Hospital affiliated to	...	Military Hospital, York.
Commandant ...	...	The Lady Holden of Alston.
Medical Officer	... Dr. W. W. Stainthorpe, Guisbrough.	
Matron ...	...	Mrs. Stainthorpe (Honorary).
Quartermaster	...	The Lord Holden of Alston.
Staffed by ...	...	Yorks./26 and Trained Nurses.

Chaloner Hall in New Road, Guisborough was built in 1881 as a Sunday School. It was loaned as a Red Cross Auxiliary Hospital by Lord Gisborough. The Commandant was Lady Holden of Alston whose husband Lord Holden rented Guisborough Hall from the Chaloner family on a 99 year lease. Previously they had lived in Nun Appleton Hall in York. Lord Holden was recorded by the Red Cross as the Quartermaster but he went away to do war work.

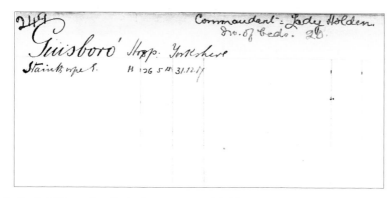

The Medical Officer, Dr. Stainthorpe was a highly regarded doctor in Guisborough. His wife was the honorary matron of the hospital, being a trained nurse, and her record card can be seen above.

Colonel Chaloner refunded the cost of coal used at the hospital which was £54-16s-0d in the Red Cross 1915 report. It was reported in the Middlesbrough Daily Gazette of 8th August 1914 that a collection from Guisborough Church services was given to Red Cross to fit up a temporary hospital to be ready when required for the sick and wounded soldiers. At one time 8000 troops were billeted in Guisborough. The hall has recently been demolished and there is now a block of flats on the site.

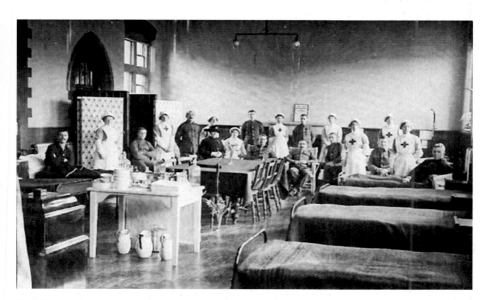

Soldiers and nurses in the Hall.

Soldiers and
nurses in the
Hall.

Daisy Ward (Armstrong) was a nurse who served at the Applegarth Camp and at the Chaloner Hall Hospital. She was given 3 uniform buttons to keep by a Canadian soldier she had nursed and wrote to another soldier for 2 years until the war ended.

Another nurse at the hospital was Malmie Nixon of Redcar who is reported in the Middlesbrough Daily Gazette of 13th November 1916 as marrying a soldier Acting Sergeant J.T.Jefferson.

The nurse on the far right of this picture (with a cross on her apron) is thought to be Rose Trevor, daughter of local attorney William Charles Trevor, who was involved in the church and many charitable activities. She remained unmarried and eventually moved to Sidmouth where she died. She kept a diary of the war years and had a collection of shells from Palestine collected by her brother during his war service in that country.

The soldiers appreciated all the care they received and one, Corporal F. Fitch gave a particularly glowing report.

"I am writing on behalf of the wounded soldiers who are at present in the Red Cross Hospital, Guisborough and as several of us are leaving here in the coming week, we should like to have an opportunity of publicly expressing our appreciation of the extremely kind treatment we have received from everyone during our stay in Guisborough, and especially for the care and devotion of the doctor and the Matron who are ably assisted by members of the local Red Cross. Although only a small town, Guisborough has provided a hospital which is replete with everything necessary to the successful treatment of our wounded men and when this awful war ceases the records of the local Red Cross will be one of the brightest spots in the annals of Guisborough."

In a letter published in the Daily Gazette of Middlesbrough on 23rd November 1916 Private J. Grey and Driver A.V. Ives write " Sir, we think it is our duty to put this letter in on behalf of the work carried on by the Red Cross in Guisborough, as the treatment we have received has been first class and that the people of Guisborough ought to be proud of this hospital, and also ought to be proud of Dr Stainthorpe and Mrs Stainthorpe for the great work they are doing for the wounded soldiers, and we also thank the nurses for the good work they are doing, and the cooks for their great work, as the meals are cooked splendidly. We also thank Mrs Del Strothers for the great work she is doing in Guisborough and the Red Cross men for the good work they are doing for the wounded soldiers."

Taking the air in the garden. Note the 2 dogs and the nurse with the soldier's cap on her lap.

Sergeant Butterfield, one of the patients at Chaloner Hall, was publicly presented with the Distinguished Conduct Medal during a hospital visit to the Picture Theatre, Guisborough. It was reported in the Daily Gazette of Middlesbrough as an interesting interlude in the programme! Sergeant Butterfield was part of a company of 40 men who captured and held a German trench which was a 100 yards long for 48 hours under continuous shelling. Twenty six of these forty men died in the incident and Sergeant Butterfield was wounded.

Lord and Lady Holden were present as were several VAD nurses from the hospital. Three cheers were given after the presentation by Major Hamilton.

Red Cross nurses in 1914 at 50, Westgate, Guisborough, later Dr. Pratt's home.

Yorks./9 VAD Guisborough Men's Detachment.

The Commandant for this detachment was William Charlton and the medical officer was Dr. William Shand. The Red Cross report for 1918 stated that meetings had been held weekly for practical and theoretical work. For air raid and bombardment duty the Detachment was divided into sections.

On 23rd January 1918 Major General Sir W.G.A. Bedford K.C.B. and Major R.L. Bower C.M.G. held an inspection of the Detachment in the Priory Gardens.

In the Autumn of 1918 Dr Shand instructed a class of 26 students in ambulance work. Dr. Burnett of Saltburn examined the men and they were all successful.

The men of the Detachment subscribed the full cost of a room for their meetings and training.

Hovingham Hall Hospital

Dr Smeeton was the Commandant and Medical Officer of the hospital and his wife was the Quartermaster.

The house is unique in being entered through an enormous riding school which is approached through a large arch from the village street. Another interesting feature is the cricket ground on the front lawn which is reputed to be the oldest continually played on private cricket ground in England.

Patients at the entrance to the riding school at Hovingham Hall.

Nurse Elizabeth Sadler with her brothers.

Men and staff on the platform of the station at Hovingham. It is thought to be 1919 just before the closure of the hospital.

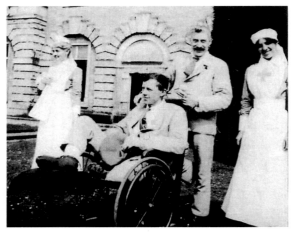

Outside Hovingham Hall with nurse Elizabeth Sadler on the left and nurse Malloy (?Hilda, ?Mary) on the right.

Sir William Worsley 3rd Baronet, who lent Hovingham Hall to the Red Cross as a hospital, with his daughters Isabel, Winifred and Victoria who were all Red Cross VAD nurses. His wife, Lady Worsley had died in 1913. Their eldest son saw military service with the Green Howards in WW1 and was a prisoner of war after being wounded. The family kept a visitors' book which all the soldiers signed as well as other visitors such as Dame Edith Sitwell.

Sample page from the visitors book.

Yorks./68. Hovingham.

Commandant and Medical Officer : Dr. C. W. Smeeton, O.B.E.

Name.	Record of War Service.	Part time or Whole time.
Borisow, Miss Edith	Hovingham Hall Red Cross Aux. Hospital	Part time
Burrell, Mrs. Blanche	,, ,,	,,
Burrell, Miss Violet G.	Lady Superintendent ,,	,,
Day, Mrs. Adeline	Hovingham Hall Red Cross Aux. Hospital	,,
Fitzwilliam, Miss Elsie	,, ,,	,,
Foster, Miss Dorothy	,, ,,	,,
Hunter, Miss Miriam	,, ,,	,,
Hunter, Miss Joan	,, ,,	,,
Ingleby, Mrs. Olivia M.	,, ,,	,,
Margan, Mrs. Gwynie	,, ,,	,,
Mallary, Miss Hilda	,, ,,	,,
Mallary, Miss Edith M.	,,	
Mothersdale, Miss Emily	,, ,,	
Magson, Miss Annie	,, ,,	,,
Magson, Miss Blanche	,, ,,	,,
Pearson, Miss Mona	,, ,,	,,
Pickett, Miss Ursula	,, ,,	,,
Tate, Mrs. Lilla	,, ,,	,,
Smeeton, Mrs. Ethel S.	,, ,,	,,
Sadler, Miss Elizabeth	,, ,,	,,
Schofield, Mrs. Margaret	,, ,,	,,
Worsley, Miss Isobel	,, ,,	,,
Colegate Mrs. Winifred	,, ,,	,,
Strickland, Miss May	,, ,,	,,
Pennyman, Miss Dorothy	,, ,,	,,
Worsley, Miss Victoria	,, ,,	,,
Colley, Miss Violet	,, ,,	,,
Tate, Miss Marion	,, ,,	,,
Tate, Miss Hilda	,, ,,	,,
Hunter, Miss Madge	,, ,,	,,
Worsley, Miss Violet	,, ,,	,,
Lascelles, Lady Isobel	,, ,,	,,
Twikey, Miss Annie	,, ,,	,,

We may write our names in albums, we may trace them in _{same}
We may chisel them on marble with a firm and skilful hand,
Soon all these will sully and the writing fades away,
Every monument will crumble, all our earthly hopes decay
But you know that there's an album filled with leaves of *snowy white*
When no page is ever tarnished, but for ever pure and *bright*
In that book of Life God's album, may your name be penned with care.
And may all who here have written, write their names for ever there.

Ste. G. G. Lawrence
A Coy,
South Wales Borderers
Pembroke Dock
South Wales.

10/12/14

Wounded at Pilckapple on
21st Oct. 1914
Only 3 Bullet Wounds.
Always Smiling.

(By Hooks or by crook I'll be
the last in this Book.
Sgt. G. Rutland
Rutland Smiles
G. Rutland.)

Extracts from the autograph book of Elizabeth Sadler

The Iron Cross.
(For German looters)

In former ferocious and barbarous times,
The thief was hung up on the cross for their crimes,
But Culture to savages offers relief —
The cross is now hung on the breast of the thief

Horringham Hall. York's 7/12/1914   (Guest).

E. Budge Sergt. 1st B. Coldstream Guards
Wounded at Langemarck, Belgium. 21st October 1914.

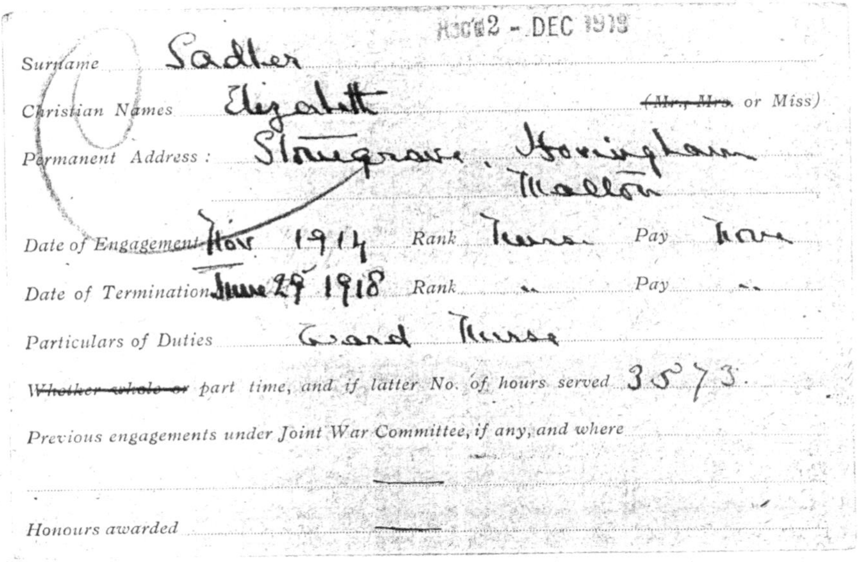

Surname Sadler

Christian Names Elizabeth (Mr. Mrs. or Miss)

Permanent Address : Stonegrave. Hovingham. Malton

Date of Engagement Nov 1914 Rank Nurse Pay none

Date of Termination June 29 1918 Rank " Pay -

Particulars of Duties Ward Nurse

Whether whole or part time, and if latter No. of hours served 3573

Previous engagements under Joint War Committee, if any, and where

Honours awarded

Elizabeth Sadler's Red Cross service card for the period, and the service card for the trained nurses at Hovingham

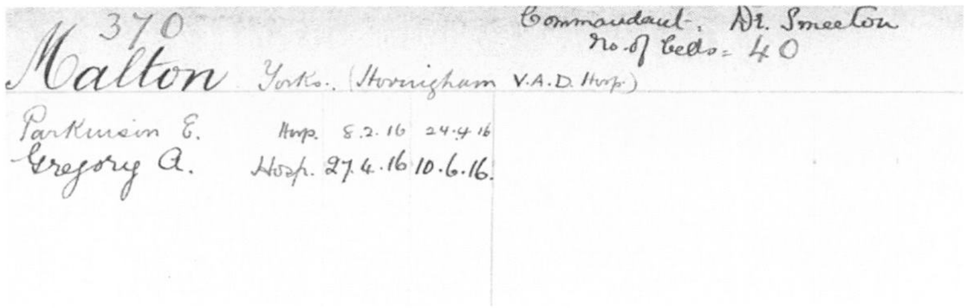

370

Malton Yorks. (Hovingham V.A.D. Hosp)

Commandant: Dr. Smeeton
No. of beds: 40

Parkinson E. Amp 8.2.16 24.4.16
Gregory A. Hosp. 27.4.16 10.6.16

94

Arncliffe Red Cross Hospital, Malton

"Arncliffe" Red Cross Hospital, Malton.

Date of opening	February 26th, 1915.
Date of closing	January 8th, 1919.
No. of Beds ...	... 23.
Total number of patients treated	500.
No. of deaths	None.
Hospital affiliated to	...East Leeds War Hospital.
Commandant	Miss Agnes Lupton.
Medical Officer	L. C. Walker, Esq., M.D., Malton.
Quartermaster	Miss Pearson.
Staffed by ...	Yorks./52 and Trained Nurses.

Arncliffe is an Edwardian townhouse on York Road in Malton. It was the family home of William Walter Lupton who was a member of a large family of wool merchants based in Leeds. Apart from owning and managing the textile and woollen mills the family were active in Leeds politics, hospital administration, patronage of the Arts and supporting other charities.

William died in 1913 and it was his daughter Agnes who offered the house to the Red Cross as a hospital during the war and acted as the Commandant there for the duration. She was 39 years old at the onset of the war. Her brother Norman was an artist and

they both also collected art. In 1952 he and Agnes donated their entire collection which contained priceless Rembrandts and watercolours by Turner and John Sell Cotman amongst many others to Leeds Art Gallery. After the war Agnes and Norman moved to Dorchester in Dorset. The Lupton family are the paternal ancestors of the Middleton family with the Duchess of Cambridge a present day descendant. The house is now in private ownership.

The quickest way to get the latest war news was to go to Malton railway station where information was tapped out on the Morse telegraph. It was only intended to be used for company business but in quiet periods the operators would relay the latest war news from York.

A Nurse's Story
Sarah Edith Hornsey nursed at Malton and at the Colchester Military Hospital. She was discharged from the Colchester Hospital in 1917 having become medically unfit to work. Sadly she died at home in Malton a year later on 31st May 1918 aged 34, from cerebrospinal fever according to her death certificate. This was most likely a meningococcal infection which was particularly virulent in crowded situations such as army barracks, at the Front and in the hospitals. It affected those who were already vulnerable such as the stressed, fatigued and ill soldiers. Sarah would have been at risk as she worked in close proximity with these men.

Her death is commemorated on the war memorial in Malton and on the Honour board in St Michael's Church.

A Patient's Story
Alfred Reginald Marshall was 19 years old when he enlisted in the Rifle Regiment of the 8TH Battalion London Regiment. He received his call up papers in August 1914 and was wounded twice, once in June 1915 and then more seriously in October 1915 when he was reported as dangerously ill with a gunshot wound to the chest. He was finally reported to be recuperating at Arncliffe Hospital Malton around February 1916. He was transferred to the Army reserve in August 1917.

Christmas at Arncliffe Hospital 1917
(taken from Journal of Leeds Territorial Hospitals 1918
"Arncliffe York Road, Malton. The festivities at the above hospital began on Christmas Eve when all the patients who were up attended an entertainment and Christmas tree given by a lady in the neighbourhood. The hospital was gaily decorated with flags and evergreens. The patients dined off turkey and plum pudding on Christmas Day, and in the evening amusements were a whist drive, games, music and refreshments being served during the evening. The patients attended a special performance at the local picture house in the afternoon. They received several presents kindly given by people in the neighbourhood and all entered enthusiastically into the amusements provided."

The Swinton and Malton Men's Detachment (Yorks./23 VAD) had Major Clive Behrens as Commandment and Dr. J.C. Walker as medical officer. During 1918 the men transported 130 soldiers to Arncliffe Hospital from Malton station. The Detachment was also in a state of readiness in case of danger from raids by hostile aircraft having men on duty every evening. At the request of the military authorities at York a journey was undertaken with the motor ambulance to remove a patient from the RAF landing ground at Grimstone Grange to Malton Cottage Hospital, entailing a journey of 32 miles.

Yorks./52. Malton.

Commandant : Miss A. Lupton

Name.	Record of War Service.	Part time or Whole time.
Lupton, Miss Agnes	Commandant. Arncliffe A. M. Hospital, Malton	Whole time
Proctor, Miss Janet	Quartermaster. Tigne Military Hospital, 6 months ; Arncliffe A. M. Hospital	Whole time / Part time
Taylor, Miss Helen	Arncliffe A. M. Hos., Feb. 1915, to Sep., 1915 (part) ; British Hos., Alexandria. Oct., 1915, to April, 1916 ; Plymouth Mil. Hos., May, 1916, to May, 1917 ; 10th General Hos., Rouen, May. 1917, to May, 1919	Whole time
Brown, Mrs. Sarah	Arncliffe A. M. Hospital	Part time
Buckle, Miss Annie	Arncliffe A. M. H., Feb.. 1915, to Sept., 1915 (part) ; British Hos., Alexandria, Oct., 1915, to Oct., 1916 ; 2nd Northern Gen. Hos., Leeds (masseuse), 2 years	Whole time
Buckle. Miss Edith	Arncliffe A. M. Hospital	Part time
Battle, Miss Ella	Arrcliffe A. M. Hospital (part) ; Redburn War Hospital, Eastbourne, Feb. to Aug., 1918 ; Hoole Bank Hospital, Chester, Aug. to Oct , 1918	Whole time
Channon, Mrs. Helen U.	Arncliffe A. M. Hospital, Feb., 1915, to Feb., 1919	Part time
Clarke, Miss Florence	,, ,,	,,
Cooper, Miss Edythe	,, ,,	,,
Dodsworth, Mrs. Elizabeth A.	,, ,, Feb., 1915, to Oct., 1917	,,
Forsyth, Mrs. Dorothea	,, ,,	,,
Glover, Miss Elizabeth	Heavy Woollen Mil. Hospital, Dewsbury, 1 year	Whole time
Halton, Mrs. Gertrude	Arncliffe A. M. Hospital, Feb., 1915, to Feb , 1919	Part time
Harding. Miss Mary	,, ,,	,,
Harding. Miss Dorothy	,, ,, Oct., 1916, to Feb., 1919	,,
Hopkins, Miss Annie	,, ,,	,,
Ingham, Miss Hylda	,, ,, Feb., 1916, to Feb., 1919	,,
Micklethwaite, Miss Janet	,, ,, Oct. 1916. to Feb , 1919	,,
Pearson, Miss Irene	,, ,, Feb., 1915, to Feb., 1919	,,
Potter, Miss Mabel	,, ,, Feb., 1915, to Oct., 1917	,,
Proctor, Miss Kathleen	,, ,, (part) ; Alnwick War Hospital as masseuse, 1 year ; Reading War Hos. as masseuse, 1 year	Whole time
Purchas, Miss Gwendoline	Arncliffe A. M. Hospital, May, 1918, to Feb , 1919	Part time
Rowntree, Miss Edith	,, ,, Feb., 1915, to Feb., 1919	,,
Russell, Miss Helen B.	,, ,, ,, ,,	,,
Russell, Miss Maud	,, ,, ,, ,,	,,
Russell, Mrs. Winifred	,, ,, May. 1916. to Feb., 1919	,,
Russell, Miss Marjorie	,, ,, Dec., 1917, to Feb., 1919	,,
Suddaby, Miss Adelaide	,, ,,	,,
Taylor, Miss Kathleen	,, ,, May, 1918, to Feb., 1919	,,
Tobey, Miss Hilda	,, ,, Feb., 1915, to Feb., 1919	,,
Clarke, Miss Kate	,, ,,	,,
Lufe, Miss May	,, ,, Feb., 1915, to Feb., 1919	,,
de Mirimonde, Mrs. Jane	,, ,,	,,

Masham Red Cross Hospital

The Red Cross Hospital, Masham, Yorks.

Building lent by	...	The Rt. Hon. Lord Masham.
Date of opening	... ...	17th January, 1918.
Date of closing	... ...	31st May, 1919.
No. of Beds ...	... ...	... 40.
Total number of patients treated	... ...	266.
No. of deaths	... ...	None.
Hospital affiliated to	...	... Military Hospital, York.
Commandant ...	... ...	The Lady Masham.
Medical Officer	.. Alfred Brown, Esq., M.B., Masham.
Quartermaster	... ...	Miss Edmundson.
Staffed by	...	Yorks./18, Trained Nurses and Masseuse.

Masham Town Hall is an impressive Grade 2 listed stone building built in 1912 and opened in May 1913 following a legacy from 2nd Lord Masham.

The hall is still in use today in the busy, historic market town set in the Yorkshire Dales.

Yorks./18. Bedale.

Commandant : Lady Beresford Peirse, O.B.E.

Medical Officer - Dr. Alan Hansell.

Name.	Record of War Service.	Part time or Whole time.
Beresford Peirse, Lady Henrietta	Commandant. Bedale Red Cross Hospital	Part time
Kirby, Miss Maud	Asst. Commandant.	Half time
Beresford-Peirse, Miss Mary	Quartermaster.	Part time
Hansell, Dr. Alan	Medical Officer.	..
Thornton, Mr.	Pharmacist.	No duty
Ackroyd, Miss Catherine	Masham Red Cross Hospital	Part time
Abbott, Mrs. Mary	Bedale Red Cross Hospital	Occasional
Atkinson, Miss Catherine	Bedale and Masham Hospitals	Part time
Bell, Miss Mildred	Bedale Hospital	,,
Brown, Miss Catherine	,,	,,
Courage, Mrs. Beatrice	,, ,,	,,
Coore, Mrs. Evelyn	,,	,,
Dobby, Miss Gertrude	,, ,,	,,
Dobby, Miss Annie	Bedale and Military Hospital, Catterick	,,
Deighton, Mrs. Annie Maude	Masham Hospital	,,
Eddison, Mrs. Constance	Bedale Hospital	,,
Edmundson, Miss Emma	Bedale and Masham Hospitals	,,
Edgar, Mrs. Margaret	,, ,, ,,	,,
Fife, Mrs. Aileen	Bedale Hospital	,,
Fothergill, Miss Grace	Bedale, 13 months ; and 1st Northern Gen. Hosp., Newcastle-on-Tyne	,,
Fothergill, Miss Maud	Bedale, St. Thomas's, Rouen, and Roehampton	Whole & part
Gray, Miss Edith Cresswell	Bedale Hospital	Part time
Gray, Miss Irene Cresswell	,, ,,	,,
Gray, Miss Margarita Cresswell	,, ,,	,,
Gibson, Mrs. Elsie	,, ,,	,,
Gent, Miss Ethel	Bedale and Masham	,,
Hood, Miss Margaret	Bedale Hospital	,,
Hare, Mrs. Margaret	,, ,,	,,
Halfpenny, Miss Maud	,, ,,	,,
Heywood, Miss Jane	,, ,,	,,
Ingleby, Miss Natalie	Bedale and Masham	,,
Kirby, Miss Rose	Bedale Hospital	,,
Learoyd, Miss Alice Nelson	,, ,,	,,
Linscott, Miss Elsie	,, ,,	,,
McDonie, Miss Harriet	,, ,,	,,
Musgrave, Miss Emily	,, ,,	,,
Maister, Miss Gladys	Masham Hospital	,,
McIntyre, Miss Ellen	Bedale Hospital	,,
McIntyre, Miss Josephine	,, ,,	,,

Name.	Record of War Service.	Part time or Whole time.
•Mace, Miss Alice	Bedale Hospital	Part time
Nicholson, Miss Florence	,, ,,	,,
Newton, Miss Harriet M.	Masham	,,
Pearson, Miss Annie	Bedale Hospital	,,
Peacock, Miss Rachel	,, ,,	,,
Pallin, Miss Greta	Bedale and Red Barns, Redcar	Whole time
Beresford-Peirse, Miss Dorothy	Bedale, Tunbridge Wells, and St. Dunstan's	Part time
Pinkney, Miss Edith	Bedale	,,
Park, Miss Margaret	Bedale, Saltburn, and Welburn Hall	,,
Pattison, Mrs. Isabella	Bedale Hospital	,,
Pauling, Miss Marie	General Hospital, London, Connaught Hospital, Aldershot	Whole time
Springett, Miss Guglielma	Bedale Hospital	Part time
Towler, Miss Milicent	,, ,,	,,
Theakston, Miss Dora	Masham Hospital	,,
Weeler, Mrs. Susan	,,	,,
Wood, Miss Cecil	Bedale	,,
Whitton, Miss Mary	,,	,,
Whitton, Miss Annie	,,	,,
Wheldon, Miss Mary		,,
Watson, Miss Ethel J.	Masham	,,
Wandesforde, Miss Maud Prior	Bedale and The Grove, Harrogate	,,
Wright, Miss Sarah	Bedale Hospital	,,
Webster, Miss Dorothy Steer	Bedale and War Hospital, Dustan, Northants	,,

Patients and staff outside the hall.

100

Priory Red Cross Hospital, Middleham

"The Priory Red Cross Hospital," Middleham.

Date of opening	October 15th, 1914.
Date of closing	February 19th, 1915.
No. of Beds	... 12.
Total number of patients treated	27.
No. of deaths	None.
Hospital affiliated to	Military Hospital, York.
Commandant	... Mrs. Topham.
Medical Officer	George Cockcroft, Esq., M.D., Middleham.
Staffed by	Yorks./58 and Trained Nurse.

This small Hospital rendered good work in the very early days of the War, when the first rush of wounded Belgian Soldiers arrived in this Country.

The Priory, believed to have been built in the 18th Century, was used as a hospital for just four months at the beginning of the war responding to the need for extra beds to care for the influx of Belgian soldiers. By the end of the war, 15,000 Belgian soldiers had been sent to England for treatment.

The 27 treated at the Priory were brought into the building secretly through a small door in the rear garden wall to avoid local people witnessing their arrival.

The Priory can be seen to the right of the church

Yorks./58. Middleham.

Commandant   Mrs. Topham.
Medical Officer :   Dr. Geo. Cockcroft.

Name.	Record of War Service.	Part time or Whole time
Beswick, Mrs. Jane	Middleham Red Cross Hospital	Part time
Chaplio, Mrs. Mary Beatrice	,, ,,	,,
Elliott, Miss Emma	,, ,,	,,
Gilham, Miss Mary Elizabeth	,, ,,	,,
Hammond, Mrs. Mildred	Bedale Hospital	,,
Herritage, Mrs. Isobel	Middleham Red Cross Hospital	,,
Kirkbride, Mrs. Mary	,, ,,	,,
Maughan, Miss Nancy	,, ,,	,,
Peacock, Miss Martha	,, ,,	,,
Pratt, Miss Emily	,, ,, and Bedale	,,
Parrish, Miss Jenny	,, ,,	,,
Paule, Mrs. Laura	,, ,,	,,
Topham, Mrs. Edith	,, ,,	,,
Wood, Mrs. Lily	,, ,, and Bedale	,,

The soldiers were cared for by members of Yorks / 58 detachment which was registered in April 1914 with Mrs. Topham of The Deanery in Middleham as their Commandant. The men were members of the Yorks/25 detachment under Col. Hammond C.B. of Middleham as Commandant, who also served as a District Representative.

Upkeep of the hospital from 15th October to 31st December 1914 amounted to £78 – 5s – 11d.

Holgate Hospital, Middlesbrough

The Red Cross Hospital, Holgate, Middlesbrough.

Building lent by ...	The Middlesbrough Board of Guardians	
Date of opening ..	...	... 1st October, 1917.
Date of closing ...	...	... 30th April, 1919.
No. of Beds ...	...	... 51.
Total number of patients treated	...	... 688.
No. of deaths ...	...	... 18.
Hospital affiliated to	...	Newcastle Genera. Hospital
Commandant ...	...	Mrs. May Hedley, O.B.E.
Medical Officer ...	...	Dr. Body, Middlesbrough.
Quartermaster ...	...	... Mrs. Gains.
Staffed by ...	...	Yorks./32 and Trained Nurses.

This Hospital was established by special request of the D.D.M.S., Northern Command, for the treatment of Sick Troops stationed in the district, and proved invaluable to the large number of men who received treatment during the two years it was open. '

In August 1914 beds were set up at Marton Road School to receive injured or ill soldiers. This arrangement was then moved to the hall in the Friends Meeting House, and subsequently to a large house in Southfield Road which was lent by Mrs. Barnley. Beds were also set up for a time in the waiting room of the" up" platform of the North East Railway Station.

Soldiers were conveyed to the various hospitals by the men who were members of the 29th Yorks. V.A.D. Middlesbrough. This detatchment, under the leadership of Dr. G.F. Longbotham, had been appointed by the War Council to deal with all cases of wounded

soldiers sent to Middlesbrough, as well as victims of accidents which were common in the works. The Detachment handled almost 4,000 cases "with devotion and self sacrifice", and were supported by the purchase of an Ambulance Van which was bought by public subscription. Another Ambulance was later gifted to them by Mr. Morley (of roundabout fame) as a mark of his appreciation of their work.

In August 1917 Mrs. Hedley of Cleveland Lodge, Middlesbrough was asked, as the District Representative of the Red Cross, to prepare a hospital "for the reception of the sick of the Tees Garrison and men who became ill whilst on leave"

Yorks./76. Middlesbrough.

Commandant: Mrs. Northfell.
Commandant during War: Mrs. Curry.

Name.		Record of War Service.				Part time or Whole time.
Northfell, Mrs. Louie	...	Commandant. Eaglescliffe, Saltburn, & Holgate (M'bro) Hosp.				Part time
Gleadhill, Miss Dora	...	Quartermaster.	,,	,,	,,	,,
Coxon, Mrs. Emma	...	Eaglescliffe, Saltburn and Holgate (Middlesbrough) Hospitals ...				,,
Corner, Mrs. Rosaline	...	,,	,,	,,	,,	,,
Conly, Mrs. Annie	...	,,	,,	,,	,,	,,
Coulton, Miss Lilly	...	,,	,,	,,	...	,,
Brown, Miss Grace	...	,,	,,	,,	...	,,
Blakeston, Miss Gladys	...	,,	,,	,,	...	,,
Edwards, Mrs. Emily	...	,,	,,	,,	...	,,
Dean, Miss Ida	...	,,	,,	,,	...	,,
Gilbraith, Miss Hannah	...	,,	,,	,,	...	,,
Gatenby, Miss Madge	...	,,	,,	,,	...	,,
Hann, Mrs. Margaret	...	,,	,,	,,	...	,,
Hogg, Mrs. Elsie M.	...	,,	,,	,,	...	,,
Hearn, Miss Florence	...	,,	,,	,,	...	,,
Harland, Mrs. Mary J.	...	,,	,,	,,	...	,,
Lille, Miss Louisa	...	,,	,,	,,	...	,,
Moss, Miss Annie	...	,,	,,	,,	...	,,
Nimmo, Miss Elsie	...	,,	,,	,,	...	,,
Pickering, Miss Harriet	...	,,	,,	,,	...	,,
Robinson, Mrs. Margaret	...	,,	,,	,,	...	,,
Roe, Miss Florence	...	,,	,,	,,	...	,,
Shields, Mrs. Lily	...	,,	,,	,,	...	,,
Spills, Mrs. Florence	...	,,	,,	,,	...	,,
Telford, Miss Mary	...	,,	,,	,,	...	,,
Walton, Miss Annie	...	,,	,,	,,	...	,,
Walton, Miss Katharine	...	,,	,,	,,	...	,,
Waggott, Mrs. Margaret	...	,,	,,	,	...	,,
Webster, Miss Margaret	...	,,	',	,,	...	,,
Elliott, Miss Ethel	...	,,	,,	,,	...	,,
Goult, Miss Alice M.	.	,,	,,	,,	...	,,

Yorks/32. Middlesbrough.

Commandant: Mrs. Hedley, O.B.E.
Medical Officer: Dr. Thos. Body.

Name.	Record of War Service.	Part time or Whole time.
Hedley, Mrs. May, O.B.E.	Commandant. Holgate Anx Mil. Hospital, Middlesbro'	Whole time
Byland, Miss Mabel	Cairo, London, etc.	,,
Jones, Miss Enid	Middlesbro', Kent, Great Hermitage	,,
Stevenson, Miss Flose	London and Paris	,,
Stephenson, Miss Dorothy	Holgate Hospital	Part time
Levett, Miss Molly	North Ormesby Hospital and Holgate Hospital	Part time
Dawson, Miss Gertrude	Etherley Hospital	Whole time
Scotson, Miss Margaret	Hemlington, Stonebridge, and Holgate	,,
Jervelund, Miss Winifred	Newcastle Military Hospital	,,
Hayham, Mrs. Catherine	Hemlington, Holgate (part) and Catterick	,,
Hedley, Mrs. Margaret	Holgate	Part time
Harvey, Miss Margaret	Hermitage, Kent, and Netley	Whole time
Cooper, Miss Ethel	Several London Hospitals	,,
Walker, Miss Louisa Maria	Regent Park Hospital, London	,,
Winterschladen, Miss Nellie Mabel	Holgate	Part time
Earp, Miss Ada	Stonebridge	Whole time
Ensoll, Miss Grace	Holgate	Part time
Ensoll, Miss Lottie	Holgate	Part time
James, Mrs. Ethel	Holgate	Part time
Gains, Mrs.	Quartermaster, Holgate Hospital	Whole time

By then known as Holgate Hospital, the large detached building was part of the Middlesbrough Union Workhouse which had been built in 1878 to accommodate 700 paupers, and was now deemed to be " in every respect a most suitable place and well adapted for a hospital". The Guardians and their officials did all in their power to help, and many of the leading firms in Middlesbrough gave considerable financial support.

Comdt. Mrs. Hedley
60 beds

98. Middlesbrough. RX Hospital

Sturges Ada. SC 11.10.17 19.1.18
Cameron Nellie M.M. 3.11.17 23.8.18
Turner Lucy 19.1.18 30.4.19
Mackay May S. JC 22.1.18 9.2.18
McKenzie Johnful JC 20.2.18 21.9.18
Bacon Nellie 13.9.18 19.12.18
Smith Mrs. Rachel JC 21.9.18 21.12.18
Copley Martha E. JC 21.12.18 21.1.19
Roberts Lizzie M. JC 23.1.19 30.4.19

The Daily Gazette for Middlesbrough reported on 15th May 1918 that "an upright grand piano was presented to the Holgate Hospital as a result of a whist drive (£28 – 12s) and concert given by Mrs Coverdale (£53 – 2s – 6d.) Money was also raised for the 'fresh air fund' for patients during summer."

A concert had previously been given by patients the night before, arranged and conducted by Airman Harman Burnett RAF who wrote a topical song which was very much applauded and appreciated as it dealt with the hospital staff and consequently created much amusement. Mrs Gains, the Quartermaster was responsible for arranging costumes. Nurse Gettins, a soprano, also sang.

It was reported as a very successful evening, concluded by an excellent little speech made by Sister Cameron.

Opened in October 1917 the hospital 'rendered most excellent service' to almost 700 patients, many severely ill, and a large proportion of them with pneumonia. It continued until the Garrison was moved from the neighbourhood, the last patient leaving at the beginning of May 1919.

As can be seen in the record card above, there were considerably more trained nurses employed here than was usual in the auxiliary hospitals.

The workhouse later became Middlesbrough General Hospital and when this building was demolished, the hospital was moved to the James Cook University Hospital site.

Mulgrave Castle

Mulgrave Hospital was donated as a Red Cross hospital by the 3rd Marquis of Normanby, married to Gertrude Stansfield Forster, the Commandant of the hospital.

The Marchioness can be seen here wearing her Commandant's uniform.

Charles Dickens is reputed to have been friends with the 2nd Marquis of Normanby visiting Whitby in 1861 and dedicating his book, 'Dombey and Son' to the Marchioness.

Yorks./68. Mulgrave and Lythe.

Commandant : The Marchioness of Normanby, O.B.E.
Quartermaster : Rev. The Marquis of Normanby.

Name.	Record of War Service.	Part time or Whole time.
Normanby, Marchioness of	Dec., 1914—May, 1919. Mulgrave Castle Aux. Mil Hos.	Whole time
Normanby, Rev. The Marquis of	"	Whole time
Barrett, Miss Florence Alice	"	Part time
Brett, Mrs. Elizabeth	April, 1915—May, 1919.	"
Carter, Mrs. Elizabeth	March, 1915—May, 1919.	"
Clarkson, Miss Ethel	Jan., 1917—May, 1919.	"
Corbett, Mrs. Jessie W. F.	March, 1915—May, 1919	"
Elders, Miss Mary A.	March, 1915—March, 1918.	"
Harland, Mrs. Clara E.	Jan. 1916—Jan. 1918.	"
Harland, Miss Dorothy M.	March, 1915—May, 1919. Mulgrave Castle Aux. Mil. Hos. ; War Hos. Huddersfield ; 4th Northern Gen. Hos., Lincoln	"
Harland, Miss Emily A.	March, 1915—May, 1919. Mulgrave Castle Aux. Mil. Hos.	"
Hutton, Mrs. Dorothy	April, 1915—May, 1919.	"
Jackson, Mrs. Mary	March, 1915—March, 1916	"
Massie, Miss Helen Mary Maud	March, 1915—May, 1919.	"
Maynard, Mrs. Hannah M.	April, 1915—April, 1916.	"
Simmons, Miss Edith E.	Feb. 1917—Feb., 1918.	Whole time
Snowdon, Miss Olive	March, 1915—Jan., 1917	Part time
Wilson, Miss Ellen	March, 1915—March, 1916.	"
Pybus, Miss Alice	April, 1915—May 1919.	"
Robinson, Mrs. Martha Jane	May, 1915—May, 1918	"

The record card of trained nurses who worked at Mulgrave Castle

The Marchioness holding their son Oswald Constantine Phipps who became the 4th Marquis of Normanby. Also in the photo are the two daughters of the Marquis and Marchioness, Lady Katherine Phipps and Lady Gertrude Phipps.

Christmas festivities at Mulgrave Castle demonstrating the efforts to entertain the soldiers.

The Nursing Staff

Northallerton Red Cross Hospital

The County Hall Red Cross Hospital, Northallerton.

Building lent by	The North Riding County Council.
Date of opening	October 15th, 1914.
Date of closing	January 10th, 1919.
No. of Beds	65.
Total number of patients treated	1,628.
No. of deaths	2.
Hospital affiliated to	East Leeds War Hospital.
Commandant	W. Baigent, Esq., M.D., M.B.E.
Assistant Commandant	Miss E. M. Stead.
Medical Officer	W. Baigent, Esq., M.D., M.B.E., Northallerton.
Matrons	Misses Norris, Wilson and Broadley.
Quartermaster	Mrs. W. Baigent.
Staffed by	Yorks./30 and Trained Nurses.

The Commandant, Dr William Baigent was a Northallerton medical officer who graduated as a doctor from Newcastle upon Tyne, studying at the Durham College of Medicine there. He was an accomplished hand tier of fishing flies and became famous for his invention of a new fly fishing bait which was named the "Baigent Brown." Jane Thornton Baigent, his wife, was a VAD nurse at the hospital and also took on the role of Quartermaster.

Dr Baigent was awarded an MBE for his work at the hospital during the war. It was reported in the Red Cross Journal of February 1918 that both Dr Baigent and Dr Mason were elected Honorary Life Members of the British Red Cross Society having given five complete courses of British Red Cross lectures gratuitously.

Photo of men and women VAD Detachment members and soldiers in the grounds of County Hall.

The men's detachment was led by Mr F. Hutton with 32 members in 1914. By 1918 the Detachment was led by Dr H. Mason.

Minute Report Book of the North Riding County Council recording discussions about the use of County Hall as a hospital and the alterations that needed to be made to accommodate the soldiers and provide entertainment. All this was done with significant cost issues.

The Chairman of the County Council reported that since the last quarterly Meeting of the Committee he had given permission for a bath, for the use of the Red Cross Hospital, to be put in the small upstairs room at the end of the South corridor, at the expense of the Red Cross ; and that he had sanctioned the use, by the wounded soldiers only, of the grounds at the South side of the County Hall for playing croquet and bowls.

H. BERESFORD-PEIRSE,
Chairman.

Northallerton, 12th July, 1915.

The New Wing at the North end of the County Hall has been completed and is now occupied.

Owing to the occupation of the Committee rooms by the Red Cross Hospital an increased supply of hot water is required and the small boiler used during the summer months is inadequate ; an estimate for improving the supply for the sum of £76 10s. 0d. has been accepted and the Red Cross Hospital have undertaken to contribute £40 towards the cost.

A tender for painting and distempering four of the offices in the original part of the North wing at the County Hall for the sum of £16 10s. 0d. has been accepted.

An arrangement has been made for providing an extension Post Office telephone to the Small Holdings Department through the Clerk of the Peace's Department.

H. BERESFORD-PEIRSE,
Chairman.

Northallerton, 10th July, 1916.

564   12th May, 1915.

The Chairman of the County Council reported that since the last Meeting of the County Council he had given permission for the holding of the Quarter Sessions in the County Hall, and also for the holding of the County Licensing Committee Meeting on the 3rd May, and had sanctioned the fixing by the Red Cross Society, at their expense, of a cooking range and a sink in the basement of the County Hall, for the use of the Red Cross Hospital.

Should the Representation of the People Bill now before Parliament become law provision will have to be made in the County Hall for the extra clerical staff that will be required by the Clerk of the County Council.

An extra cooking stove has been fixed by the Red Cross Hospital in their kitchen in the basement of the County Hall, and a washing-up sink has been fixed by them in the South corridor upstairs and hot and cold taps in the bathroom ; these additions were approved by the Committee.

H. BERESFORD-PEIRSE,
Chairman.

Northallerton, 14th January, 1918.

Elizabeth Lyall was a district nurse in the Goole area who married William Hay in 1899. After their marriage they moved to Northallerton where they bought the grocery business at 10 South Parade. Elizabeth supported the soldiers in County Hall by making teacakes for them, no doubt a tasty treat appreciated by the men!

Picture of nurses and soldiers in one of the adapted committee rooms.

The photo was given by John Hutton the then Chairman of the North Riding County Council.

North Riding County Council School Offices, Northallerton.   No. 1554.

Postcard of County Hall sent by a patient, Reg Downing, describing the hospital and the fact that the local government offices of the North Riding continued to be based there.

Yorks/30. Northallerton.

Commandant and Medical Officer : W. Baigent, Esq., M.D., M.B.E.

Name.	Record of War Service.	Part time or Whole time.
Stead, Miss Edith	Asst. Commandant. Northallerton Red Cross Aux. Hospital ...	Whole time
Stead, Miss Hilda Yeoman	Northallerton Red Cross Aux. Hospital, No. 1 N.Z. General ...	,,
Baigent, Mrs. Jane	,, ,, ,, ...	Part time
Bell, Mrs. Marian	,, ,, ,, ...	,,
Atlay, Mrs. Florence	,, ,, ,, ...	,,
Baines, Miss Agnes	,, ,, ,, ...	,,
Bower, Miss Ada	,, ,, ,, ...	,,
Beale, Miss Louie	,, ,, ,, ...	,,
Brockhill, Miss Mabel	Northallerton Aux. Hos. ; Royal Naval Hos.. Portland ; still serving Royal Naval Hospital, Chatham ...	,,
Constantine, Miss Margarita	Northallerton Red Cross Aux. Hospital, No. 1 N Z. General ...	,,
Cox, Miss Sarah	,, ,, ,, ...	,,
Eaton, Mrs. Minnie	,, ,, ,, ...	,,
Eaton, Miss Madge	Northallerton Aux. Hos. ; 1st East General, Cambridge ; 55th General, B.E.F. ...	,,
Fairburn, Mrs. May	Northallerton Red Cross Aux. Hospital ...	,,
Fairburn, Mrs Jemima	,, ,, ,, ...	,,
Greer, Miss Ada	,, ,, ,, ...	,,
Gibson, Mrs. May	,, ,, and Saltburn ...	,,
Gardner, Miss Grace	,, ,, ,, and oN. 1 N.Z. Gen. Hos.	,,
Guthrie, Miss Joyce	,, ,, ,, ...	,,
Squire, Miss Eva Hutton	,, ,, ,, ...	,,
Walker, Mrs. Lilas Hill	,, ,, ,, ...	,,
Jameson, Miss Annie	,, ,, ,, ...	,,
Kitching, Mrs. Florence	,, ,, ,, ...	,,
Hallimond, Mrs. Mabel	,, ,, ,, ...	,,
Naylor, Mrs. Rosina	,, ,, ,, ...	,,
Norster, Mrs. Ada	& "Red Barns" Hospital, Saltburn Hospital, Welburn Hall Hosp.	,,
Pattinson, Miss Dora	Northallerton, Richmond, and Saltburn Hospitals ...	,,
Pearson, Mrs. Emma	,, ,, ,, ...	,,
Ray, Miss Flora	,, ,, ,, and Saltburn ...	,,
Robson, Mrs. Fanny	,, ,, ,, ...	,,
Russell, Miss Hilda	,, ,, ,, ...	,,
Stead, Miss Clarice	,, ,, ,, ...	,,
Wright, Miss Emma	,, ,, ,, ...	,,
Ward, Miss Nellie	,, ,, and No. 1 East Gen., Cambridge	,,
Ward, Miss Elizabeth	Northallerton Red Cross Aux. Hospital ...	,,
Wilford, Miss Mabel	,, ,, ,, ...	,,
Willoughby, Miss Mary	,, ,, ,, ...	,,
Winch, Miss Muriel	,, ,, ,, ...	,,
Baigent, Miss Jennie	,, ,, ,, ...	,,
Colton, Mrs.	,, ,, ,, ...	,,
Naylor, Miss Margaret	,, ,, ,, and at¾ London Gen. Hos	,,
Lupton-Robinson, Mrs. May	Northallerton Red Cross Aux. Hospital ...	,,
Lister, Miss Ethel	,, ,, ,, ...	,,
Eaton, Miss Gertrude	,, ,, ,, and at Bagthorpe Mil. Hos.	,,
Clark, Miss Annie	,, ,, ,, ...	,,

Mrs Marian Bell, one of the VAD nurses in this list kept her uniform which was passed on to us by her daughter, the late Miss Marjorie Bell, and which we now use as part of our exhibition.

Military Sunday Procession in Northallerton showing the VAD nurses in the centre.

Soldiers and nurses with one soldier holding a dog. Dogs and other animals were encouraged in the hospitals to aid recovery. Note the patriotic flags on the bed linen.
The lady in the darker dress may be Mrs Baigent.

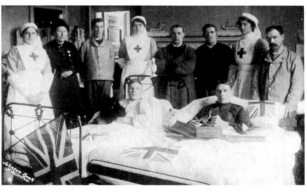

Certificates of Marian Allan from Brompton, Northallerton who was a VAD nurse at County Hall.
She completed 5184 hours of service by the end of 1917.

115

Hallgarth Red Cross Hospital, Pickering

" Hallgarth " Red Cross Hospital, Pickering.

Date of opening	1st April, 1915.
Date of closing	7th March, 1919.
No. of Beds	22.
Total number of patients treated ...	372.
No. of deaths	None.
Hospital affiliated to ...	Military Hospital, York.
Commandant	Mrs. Kirk, O.B.E.
Medical Officer	John L. Kirk, Esq., B.A., M.B., B.C., Pickering.
Quartermaster	Mrs. Pickup.
Staffed by	Yorks./34 and Trained Nurse.

One Oak, Hallgarth was established as a Red Cross Hospital for wounded soldiers. The Matron was Mrs. Noah Kirk, wife of Dr. J.L. Kirk. These premises continued to be used as a Doctor's Surgery until the present purpose built premises were opened on the Ropery.

The first batch of soldiers admitted to Hallgarth

Yorks/34. Pickering.

Commandant: Mrs. J. L. Kirk. O.B.E.
Medical Officer: Dr. J. L. Kirk.

Name.	Record of War Service.	Part time or Whole time.
Kirk, Mrs. Norah	Commandant. Hallgarth Hospital, Pickering, 1915–1919	Daily
Pickup, Mrs. Mary Jane	Quartermaster. Hallgarth Hospital, Pickering, 1916—1919	Daily
Appleby, Miss Mary	Hallgarth Hospital, Pickering	Part time
Arnett, Miss Annie	" " "	"
Armstrong, Miss Elizabeth	" " "	"
Boulton, Mrs. Mary	" " "	"
Boulton, Miss Annie	" " "	"
Bowman, Miss Annie	Pickering, York Military Hospital, and in Egypt	"
Coverdale, Miss Elizabeth	Pickering	Whole time
Cooper, Miss Christine	Pickering and E. Leeds Infirmary	Part time
Dove, Miss Eveline	Pickering	"
Dodds, Miss Edith	"	"
Foster, Miss Mary	"	"
Frank, Mrs. Hannah	"	"
Frank, Miss Frances	Pickering and Wylde Green Mil. Hospital, Birmingham	"
Gibson, Miss Phyllis	Pickering and Leeds Infirmary	"
Greenwood, Miss Jessie	Pickering	"
Hanson, Miss Florence	"	"
Hanson, Miss Ida	"	"
Highfield, Mrs. Alice	"	"
Irving, Miss Emily	"	Whole time
Johnson, Miss Madge	"	Part time
Kitching, Miss Jennie	"	"
Lund, Mrs. Alice	"	"
Lund, Miss Clara	"	"
Loy, Miss Isabel	"	"
McKenzie, Miss Margaret	"	"
Nicholson, Mrs. Violet	"	"
Riley, Mrs. Ethel	"	"
Riley, Miss Emmie	Pickering, Mil. Hospital at Halifax, and also at Cambridge	"
Scott, Miss Dorothy	Pickering and Halifax	"
Turnbull, Miss Phoebe	Pickering	"
Wills, Miss Amy	Rock Ferry Military Hospital	Whole time
Whitehead, Miss Muriel	Pickering, York Military Hospital, and in Egypt	Part time
Thompson, Mrs. Alice	Pickering	"
Wood, Mrs. Gwen	"	"
Shipman, Mrs. Jessie	"	"
Foster, Miss Annie	"	"

117

Dr Kirk in his car 'Old Reliability' ® taking part in the pageant of 1910.

Dr. Kirk's two sons both served in the war. Franklin fought at the Somme, and after recovering from shell shock, probably at Hallgarth, he returned to the Flying Corps. John fought at the Somme, Vimy Ridge and Passchendaele.

Wounded soldiers and nurses behind One Oak, Hallgarth.

The Yorks./37 VAD Men's Detachment under the command of Mr A.V. Shipman and Medical Officer Dr C.H. Toke undertook weekly practice parades. Twenty five men passed their examination in First Aid and all were equipped with regulation uniform including haversacks and water bottles.

The Detachment undertook transporting convoys of patients arriving for Hallgarth Hospital. No suitable wheeled vehicles being available, all stretcher cases had to be hand carried a considerable distance. No record was kept of the number of cases but more than 20 members had been called out on some occasions to deal with stretcher cases.

It is reported that "the work has been satisfactorily done and the patients have frequently spoken their appreciation of the careful handling by our men."

Red Barns Hospital, Redcar.

" Red Barns Hospital," Redcar.

Building lent by	Sir Hugh Bell, Bart., C.B.
Date of opening	... 9th January, 1915.
Date of closing	... 30th April, 1919.
No. of Beds ...	... 90.
Total number of patients treated	... 1,345,
No. of deaths ...' ...	... 25.
Hospital affiliated to ...	East Leeds War Hospital.
Commandant	Mrs. Claude Pease, O.B.E.
Medical Officer ...	A. S. Robinson, Esq., M.D., Redcar.
Matron	Miss Kate Emerson, A.R.R.C.
Quartermaster	... Mrs. Harald Dixon
Staffed by	Yorks./8 and Trained Nurses.

This Hospital did extremely good work not only with Overseas cases but local Troops and accidents from Marske Aerodrome.

The Ward Street Directory of 1912-13 lists the house as designed by the architect Philip Webb and built 1868 to 1870 following a commission from the Bell family.

The 1871 census lists the original inhabitants as:
Thomas Hugh Bell, ironmaster, his wife Maria and their two young children, Gertrude and Maurice, plus two relatives and six female household staff.

Amongst other positions held T. H. Bell was a Director of the Middlesbrough steel-works, and a Director of the North Eastern Railway. The siting of Red Barns, with the existing Middlesbrough to Saltburn railway line at the bottom of his garden, allowed him to have a private platform.

The 1905 Kelly Directory lists the Bell family as still living at Red Barns but some time that year they left, and moved permanently to the family home at Rounton Grange (also designed by Webb) at East Rounton.

H Dixon, ship builder (of Raylton Dixon & Co, Middlesbrough) then became the resident of Red Barns. His father had served as a County Magistrate and Tees Conservancy Commissioner with T H Bell.

Redcar Urban District Council Minutes of September 3rd 1914 note that Captain Harald Dixon of Red Barns wrote to thank them for the use of a room in the Council offices as a recruiting office.

The London Gazette of 13th October 1914 published that Harald Raylton Dixon (late Captain, 1st Volunteer Battalion, The Durham Light Infantry) (temporary) became a Captain of the 4th Battalion, Alexandra, Princess of Wales's Own (Yorkshire Regiment) on 10th September 1914. Within days (September 13th) he wrote to the Council informing them that he was "leaving Red Barns on September 30th so that it can be turned into a Red Cross Hospital". He asked for a reduction in the water rate "as I shall have the management of the finances of the hospital". The next Council reference is on November 1st 1917 when it is recorded that a "letter of thanks for a reduced water rate is received from Mrs Lucy Pease, Commandant Auxiliary Military Hospital, Red Barns". Around the same date Mrs Pease is given permission to use the mortuary in Pierson Street.

In 1916 Gertrude Bell, daughter of the house, was asked to go to the Middle East and help with mapping the land and tribes, aiding liaison between them during the war. On one of her travels over there she met a Colonel Crossley who had been 2 years in Richmond, North Riding, teaching and examining many of the Red Cross Detachments and attended a Field Day in 1912. There is a beautiful window in East Rounton Church which celebrates her achievements.

The Council proposal to place a plaque commemorating Gertrude Bell was agreed by Coatham School Governors in 1934 and can be seen on the Kirkleatham Street frontage to this day. Gertrude worked for the Red Cross in London and France indexing missing, wounded and dead soldiers so that their relatives could be informed, an early example of the tracing service undertaken by British Red Cross which still does valuable work today.

Surname	**BELL,**		Rec'd 8 JUL 1918	
Christian Names	**(Miss) Gertrude Lowthian,**		(Mr., Mrs. or Miss)	
Permanent Address :	Rounton Grange,			
	Northallerton.			
Certificate No.	507.	Age when engaged		
Date of Engagement	8-6-18.	Rank Secty.)	Pay	
Date of Termination	8-10-18.	Rank Secty.)	Pay	

Previous engagements under Joint War Committee, if any, and where

Dept. for Reference **Wounded & Missing.**

Honours awarded

	PERIOD OF SERVICE, Etc.	
From 3-6-18. To 8-10-18.	Commission or Department or County	France.
	Hon. . Coventry. Personnel.	

120

Yorks./8.   Redcar and Marske.

Commandant: Mrs. C. Pease, O.B.E.
Medical Officer: Dr. A. S. Robinson.

Name.	Record of War Service.	Part time or Whole time
Pease, Mrs. Claud ...	Commandant, "Red Barns," Redcar	Whole time
Dixon, Mrs. Dorothea Margaret	Quartermaster, ,, ,,	Part time
Milburne, Miss Mary ...	"Red Barns," Redcar	,,
Duncan, Mrs. Lucy ...	,, ,,	,,
Letty, Miss Eden... ...	,, ,,	,,
Robson, Miss Mary ...	,, ,,	,,
Patterson, Mrs. Mary ...	,, ,,	,,
Burns, Mrs. Eliza	,, ,,	,,
Wheat, Miss Mary	,, ,,	,,
Wilson, Mrs. Annie... ...	,, ,,	,,
Batty, Mrs. Lilian	,, ,,	,,
Kaye, Miss Edith... ...	,, ,,	,,
Buckley, Miss Harriet ...	,, ,,	,,
Bulmer, Miss Hilda ...	,, ,,	,,
Anderson, Miss Ella ...	,, ,,	,,
Anderson, Miss Jeannie ...	,, ,,	,,
Ridley, Miss Kathleen ...	,, ,,	,,
Petch, Miss Hannah ...	,, ,,	,,
Mackinlay, Miss Margaret ...	,, ,,	,,
Dixon, Miss Inga ...	,, ,,	,,
Sanderson, Miss Margaret ...	,, ,,	,,
Dixon, Miss Katharine ...	,, ,,	,,
Emerson, Miss Kate ...	Lady Superintendent, "Red Barns," Redcar	Whole time

Of the nursing VADs above Dorothea Margaret Dixon was the wife of Harald Dixon who lived at Red Barns and was a member of the biggest ship building family on the Tees. Dorothea was a niece of Lady Florence Bell, second wife of Sir Hugh Bell, and President of the North Riding Branch of the British Red Cross Society. Harald's sister Inga Dixon was also a VAD.

The number of patients treated is worthy of note, the hospital doing "extremely good work, not only with overseas cases, but (also) local Troops and accidents from Marske aerodrome."

From Cleveland Standard (local paper)

Dec 4th 1915 – "Redcar Red Cross get an ambulance which carries 4 stretchers, driver and an attendant."

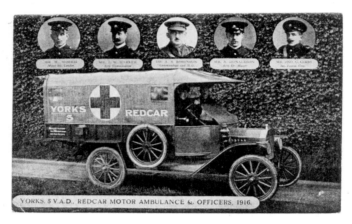

YORKS. 5 V.A.D., REDCAR MOTOR AMBULANCE & OFFICERS, 1916.

In the North Riding Red Cross financial reports for 1915 the expenditure on the motor ambulance is reported as £168-12s, licenses and insurances £18-17s-3d, petrol £8-16s-11d and motor outfits £2-14s.

Sept 15th 1917 – Commandant Marske and Redcar Detachment 8th Yorks, Mrs Claude Pease informs us that they are leaving Kirkleatham Hall and moving to Red Barns, Coatham.

Oct 27th 1917 – From the local gossip column of the paper "If we shall ever know the real truth for removing the hospital from Kirkleatham to Red Barns".

Jan 12th 1918 – Extension opened at Red Barns Auxiliary Hospital by Lady Bell. During the last 3 years Kirkleatham and Coatham Hospitals have treated over 700.

May 25th 1918 – Red Barns Hospital has 103 beds.

Daily Gazette from Middlesbrough Newspaper

23/8/15 Lady Florence Bell made presentations to Redcar and Marske Men's VAD Detachment at Redcar.

26/1/16 A Red Cross display was held at the Redcar Wesley Guild with practical demonstrations and 25 exercises carried out with the efficiency the detachment is noted for. A collection was made for Red Cross.

10/11/16 Penny Fund at Redcar "enables all classes to pay their tribute to the wounded warriors by seeing that the hospitals are adequately financed and able to provide comforts."

24/11/17 Another entertainment with popular songs, dancing, excellent humourist Corporal Jones and Corporal Wood, a patient, who amused his comrades with an up to date (too much so for some of his colleagues) ventriloquial turn!

30/11/17 "Our heroes at Red Barns have had two pleasant evenings this week. The Cleveland Quartet assisted by two patients gave a performance which was given rounds of applause, a sure token of the soldiers' gratitude"

6/12/17 A party arranged by Mrs Alderson gave the patients a most enjoyable evening. Matron and the Quartermaster offered light refreshments to Mrs Alderson and her friends.

1/6/18 Redcar Allotments Association organised weekly collections of surplus vegetables to give to the wounded men at Red Barns which had 103 men staying at that time. It was said that "if one cabbage or two or three pounds of potatoes were given by each 'knight of the spade' a respectable gift would result."

People were encouraged not only to send fruit and vegetables but to collect eggs for the national egg collection.

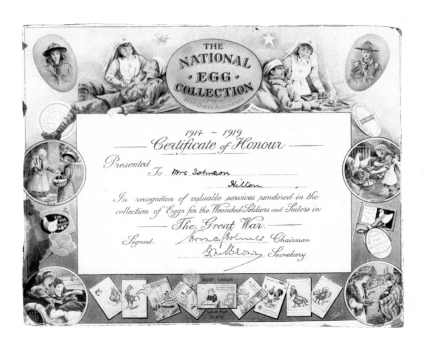

Richmond Red Cross Hospital

" Richmond Red Cross Hospital," Richmond.

Date of opening ...	...	... 16th October, 1914.
Date of closing ...	...	... 17th April, 1919.
No. of Beds ...	...	... 100.
Total number of patients treated	...	1,352.
No. of Deaths ...	...	... 2.
Hospital affiliated to	...	East Leeds War Hospital and Sunderland War Hospital.
Commandant ...	...	Miss E. Pease, O.B.E.
Assistant Commandant	...	... Miss M. Bourke.
Medical Officers ...	...	Dr. Eyres.
		Major Whitehead)
		Major Harkness } R.A.M.C.
		Major Cox)
Matron ...	...	... Miss Jane Thompson, A.R.R.C.
Quartermaster ...	...	... Mrs. G. A. Roper.
Staffed by ...	...	... Yorks./10 and Trained Nurses.

Two houses were initially used as convalescent hospitals in Richmond; Swale House, which until recently was the Richmondshire District Council headquarters and Frenchgate House. Swale House is thought to have accommodated officers and also some Belgian refugees before they were moved into agricultural occupations. It was standard practice at that time for officers and other ranks in the army to be cared for in separate hospitals.

Frenchgate House was the Red Cross Hospital for other ranks but it too looked after some Belgian refugees at the beginning of the war. The Matron, Miss Jane Thompson, was a professional nurse and has the letters A.R.R.C. after her name which stands for Associate of the Royal Red Cross, an honour bestowed upon trained nurses by the Red Cross.

Unsually there were several doctors involved in the care of patients, probably due to the close proximity of Catterick Garrison. Three of these doctors were Majors in the Royal Army Medical Corps.

An article in the Daily Gazette from Middlesbrough of 14th October 1916 reported that on the second anniversary of the hospital 295 sick and wounded soldiers had been treated during that period with good results. The Commandant, Miss Pease, had received an urgent request from Red Cross to provide 20 more beds thus providing 52 beds in total. This required the opening and furnishing of another property in Richmond, called St Agathas, as well as 2 more trained nurses. These nurses' names can be seen on the Red Cross card on p 126. The newspaper article suggested that this would be expensive and, as costs were rising, any donations in kind or money would be gratefully received. The photos suggest however that Swale House provided the extra accommodation.

The first intake of Belgian refugees.

A group of staff and patients 1916

Convalescent exercises in the garden of Frenchgate House, conducted by one of the nurses 1916

Staff and patients at Swale House, Frenchgate.

Yorks/10. Richmond.

Commandant : Miss E Pease, O.B.E.

Assistant Commandant : Miss M Bourke.

Medical Officer : Dr Eyre.

Name.	Record of War Service.	Part time or Whole time
Pease, Miss Evelyn A. ...	Commandant. 1914 to 1919, Aux. Mil. Hos., Richmond, Yorks.	Whole time
Bourke, Miss Margaret A. ...	Asst. ,, ,, ,, ,, ,,	,,
Bloomfield, Miss Katherine ...	Lady uperintendent	
Roper, Mrs. Ethel T. ...	Quartermaster. Richmond Aux. Mil. Hospital ...	Part time
Chester, Miss Kathleen ...	Richmond Aux. Mil. Hospital ·	,,
Dowson, Miss Hannah ...	,, ,,	,,
Field, Mrs. Olive ...	,, ,,	,,
Fawcett, Miss Alice ...	,, ,,	,,
Fowler Jones, Mrs. Emily ...	,, ,,	Whole time
Haw, Miss Emily...	,, ,,	Part time
Hodgson, Miss Mary	,, ,,	,,
Jones, Miss Anna ...	Scorton Hospital, Richmond Aux. Hospital	,,
Leather, Miss Doris ...	Richmond Aux. Mil. Hospital	,,
Murray, Miss Letty ...	,, ,,	,,
Muir, Mrs. Gladys	Richmond and Duchess of Westminster's, La Touquet	
Pease, Miss Mary... ...	2½ years Aux. Mil. Hospital, Richmond ; 1½ years Queen Alexandra's Hospital, Dunkirk	
Rolls, Mrs. Dorothy ...	Richmond Aux. Mil. Hospital	Part time
Royd, Miss Winifred ...	,, ,, ...	,,
Ruck-Keene, Mrs Dorothy ...	,, ,, ...	,,
Rogers, Miss Rachel ...	,, ,, ...	,,
Saunders, Mrs. Sarah ...	,, ,, ...	,,
Sayers, Mrs. Ethel ...	,, ,, ...	,,
Walton, Miss Annie ...	,, ,, ...	,,
Woddy, Mrs. Mary ...	,, ,, ...	
Turner, Miss Ethel ...	,, ,, ...	Whole time
Hodgson, Miss Annie ...	,, ,, ...	Whole time
Roper, Miss Ruth ...	,, ...	Part time
Stobart, Miss Doris ...	,, ,, ...	Whole time
Whitehead, Miss Emily ...	,, ...	Part time

A member of staff and patients the rear of Frenchgate House.

Richmond. Yorks. 472

Commandant: Mrs. Evelyn Pease.
No. of Beds: 46

Hayward. A.N.C. 2.6 29.10.15 27.1.16
Emerson Lillie J.C. 20.2.17 1.3.19
Thompson J.Y. J.C. 20.2.17 1.5.19

East Rounton Red Cross Auxiliary Hospital

"Rounton Red Cross Auxiliary Hospital,"
Rounton.

Building lent by ...	...	Sir Hugh Bell, Bart., C.B.
Date of opening ...	...	25th November, 1914.
Date of closing ...	...	3rd January, 1919.
No. of Beds ...	...	37.
Total number of patients treated	...	387.
No. of deaths ...	...	None.
Hospital affiliated to	...	Military Hospital, York.
Commandant ...	...	Lady Bell, D.B.E.
Medical Officers ...	The late Dr. Faull, Osmotherley.	
	Dr. W. Yeoman, Stokesley.	
Quartermaster ...	...	Miss D. M. Blaxland.
Staffed by ...	...	Yorks./44 and Trained Nurses.

Rounton Village Hall was designed in the Arts and Craft style by Philip Webb in 1906 at the request of Sir Hugh Bell who donated it for the use of the village. This postcard with the picture of the hospital was sent by one of the soldiers to a relative. It is interesting to note that he found it quiet. Soldiers from towns and cities were often surprised by the peaceful environment and after the noise of war it was essential in aiding their recovery.

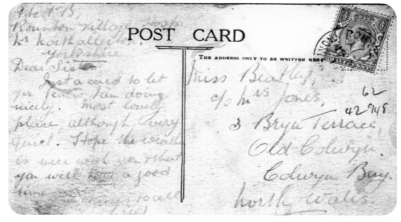

Sir Hugh Bell served on the Executive Committee of the North Riding Branch of the British Red Cross Society. He lived with his family at Rounton Grange, East Rounton. His wife Lady Florence Bell was not only President of the North Riding Branch but also Commandant of the Rounton hospital.

Florence Bell 1928

She took a personal interest in all the Detachments of the North Riding attending prize giving, parades, training camps and competitions and donated a cup to be given in her name to the winners of these competitions.

In the 3rd North Riding War Report for 1917 the County Director pays tribute to the immense amount of time and labour that she had contributed to the work of the Branch and lists her activities as:

"Commandant Yorks/44; Commandant of the Rounton Red Cross Auxiliary Hospital; Member of the Joint Women's VAD Committee, Devonshire House; Member of the Selection Board, Devonshire House; Member of the Voluntary Aid Sub-Advisory Committee; President of Sir Edward Ward's Voluntary Work Organisation; Chairman of the Women's Agricultural Committee; and Member of the Men's Agricultural Committee."

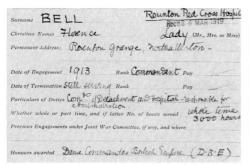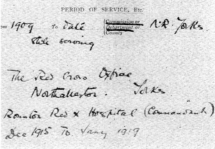

Nurses from Rounton with Lady Bell (wearing the hat) July 1919

Yorks./44. Rounton.

Commandant : Lady Bell, D.B.E.

Name.		Record of War Service.		Part time or Whole time.
Bell, Lady Florence	...	Commandant. Rounton Red Cross Hospital	...	Part time
Blaxland, Miss Dorothy	...	Quartermaster ,, ,,		,,
Barnett, Miss Gertrude	...	Rounton Red Cross Hospital ; Tonic Street, Rock Ferry, Cheshire ; Royal Herbert, Woolwich	...	Whole time Part time
Blackburn, Miss Elizabeth	.	Rounton Red Cross Hospital	...	,,
Dobson, Miss Eliza	...	,, ,,	...	,,
Elgie. Miss Edith	...	,, ,,	...	,,
Hesletine, Mrs. Mary	...	,, ,,	...	,,
Lennard, Miss Mary	..	,, ,,	...	,,
Evison, Mrs. Elizabeth	..	,, ,,	...	,,
Eskcritt, Miss Evelyn	..	,, ,,	...	,,
Batty, Miss Hilda	...	,, ,,	...	,,
Kirk, Mrs. Annie	...	,, ,,	...	,,
Metcalfe, Mrs. Elizabeth	...	,, ,,	...	,,
Constantine, Miss Elsie	...	,, ,, and Richmond, Yorks,	...	Part & Whole
Hoggarth, Miss Edith	...	,, ,,	...	Part time
Hicks, Mrs. Esther	...	,, ,,	...	,,
Pybus, Miss Annie	...	,, ,,	...	,,
Elliot, Miss Eleanor	...	,, ,,	...	,,
Robinson, Miss Elizabeth	...	,, ,,	...	,,
Stephenson, Mrs. Selina	...	,, ,,	...	,,
Robinson, Mrs. Violet	...	,, ,,	...	,,
Metcalfe, Miss Annie	...	,, ,,	...	,,
Hunt, Miss Elizabeth	...	,, ,,	...	,,
Johnson, Mrs. Dorothy	...	,, ,,	...	,,
Davies, Miss Mary	...	,, ,,	...	,,
Hicks, Mrs. H. Wayte	...	,, ,,	...	

130

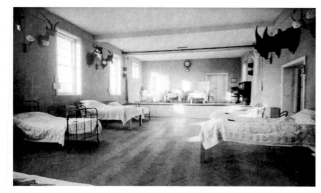

The hospital ward ready to receive the first wounded and sick soldiers.

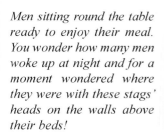

Men sitting round the table ready to enjoy their meal. You wonder how many men woke up at night and for a moment wondered where they were with these stags' heads on the walls above their beds!

The Village Hall today is at the centre of the village activities. We were privileged to be asked to recreate a WW1 hospital when it celebrated its centenary in 2006.

131

Cliffden Red Cross Hospital, Saltburn

**"Cliffden" Red Cross Hospital,
Saltburn-by-the-Sea.**

Date of opening ···	···	23rd December, 1914.
Date of closing ···	···	··· 16th August, 1919.
No. of Beds ···	···	50.
Total number of patients treated	···	1,152.
No. of deaths ···	···	1.
Hospital affiliated to	···	East Leed War Hospital.
Commandant ···	···	A. J. Longley, Esq., M.D.
Medical Officer ···	···	A. J. Longley, Esq., M.D.
Matrons ···	Miss Hextall (deceased) ; Miss Brennan.	
Secretary ···	···	··· Mr. T. Colbeck.
Staffed by ···	···	Yorks./76 and Trained Nurses.

This Hospital was originally established by Miss Robertson, but was taken over at the end of 1917 by the North Riding Branch. In May, 1919, it was lent to the Ministry of Pensions but had to be closed in August as the property was sold, and no other suitable house in the district could be found.

Situated on the east side of Saltburn Glen in the parish of Skelton and Brotton, the house was built around 1871.The first occupant was William Scope Ayrton who was a retired barrister and active judge. It is thought that that one of the earliest telephone calls in the country was made from Cliffden to Balmoral Terrace by William Ayrton to Sir Francis Fox via a line laid across the Halfpenny Bridge by Mr Irvine who was staying with Sir Francis.

After its use as a hospital it became a private house again until the second World War, when it was occupied by the ATS. It finally became a school which was demolished in the 1970s. The land is now occupied by Cliffden Court flats.

Unusually two matrons of the hospital died during their service. Margaret Jane Brennan, a trained nurse died on 22nd February 1919 during the flu pandemic which swept the world, killing more people than the war. She was buried on 25th February in an unknown location.

Elizabeth Ann Hextall who was also a matron died and is buried in Saltburn cemetery with no headstone.

There are plans to include these two matrons on a memorial to civilians who died in WW1 service.

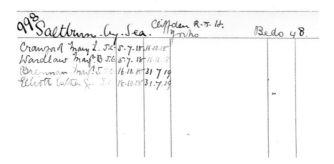

Article in the Middlesbrough Daily Gazette of the 23rd September 1916 asking for comforts for soldiers at Cliffden Red Cross Hospital.

This photo of wounded soldiers is on a postcard sent from Saltburn in April 1918 by Mary Bayley to her mother in North Ormesby. Was the soldier marked with an ink cross known to Mary and did she work at the hospital in some capacity?

Hospital ships arrived at West Hartlepool where soldiers who were not admitted to the Cameron Hospital were sent to Saltburn by train. The members of the VAD Men's Detachment, including George Hick, met them there to transport them in whicker trolleys to Cliffden. This involved a journey over the Halfpenny Bridge which was built to link Saltburn to Skelton. The bridge was a cast iron construction which had been completed in 1869 at a cost of £700 and the lives of three workmen. The 660 feet long bridge spanned the valley 120 feet above the Pleasure Grounds at its highest point. The patients and VAD members were exempt from the halfpenny toll which usually had to be paid at the booths at each end and which gave the bridge its name.

In October 1916 the Daily Gazette from Middlesbrough reported that 27 wounded soldiers were entertained at the Palace Theatre Redcar by kind permission of the manager, and supper was served at Lonsdale's café, all the arrangements being made by Saltburn Comforts Committee. On 4th December teachers and scholars at Saltburn High School for Girls entertained the soldiers at Cliffden.

Yorks./76.   Middlesbrough.

Commandant : Mrs. Northfell.
Commandant during War : Mrs. Curry.

Name.	Record of War Service.		Part time or Whole time.
Northfell, Mrs. Louie	...	Commandant. Eaglescliffe, Saltburn, & Holgate (M'bro) Hosp.	Part time
Gleadhill, Miss Dora	...	Quartermaster. ,, ,, ,,	,,
Coxon, Mrs. Emma	...	Eaglescliffe, Saltburn and Holgate (Middlesbrough) Hospitals ...	,,
Corner, Mrs. Rosaline	...	,,	,,	,,	,,
Conly, Mrs. Annie	...	,,	,,	,,	,,
Coulton, Miss Lilly	...	,,	,,	,,	,,
Brown, Miss Grace	...	,,	,,	,,	...	,,
Blakeston, Miss Gladys	...	,,	,,	,,	...	,,
Edwards, Mrs. Emily	...	,,	,,	,,	...	,,
Dean, Miss Ida	...	,,	,,	,,	...	,,
Gilbraith, Miss Hannah	...	,,	,,	,,	...	,,
Gatenby, Miss Madge	...	,,	,,	,,	...	,,
Hann, Mrs. Margaret	...	,,	,,	,,	...	,,
Hogg, Mrs. Elsie M.	...	,,	,,	,,	...	,,
Hearn, Miss Florence	...	,,	,,	,,	...	,,
Harland, Mrs. Mary J.	...	,,	,,	,,	...	,,
Lille, Miss Louisa	...	,,	,,	,,	...	,,
Moss, Miss Annie	...	,,	,,	,,	...	,,
Nimmo, Miss Elsie	...	,,	,,	,,	...	,,
Pickering, Miss Harriet	...	,,	,,	,,	...	,,
Robinson, Mrs. Margaret	...	,,	,,	,,	...	,,
Roe, Miss Florence	...	,,	,,	,,	...	,,
Shields, Mrs. Lily	...	,,	,,	,,	...	,,
Spills, Mrs. Florence	...	,,	,,	,,	...	,,
Telford, Miss Mary	...	,,	,,	,,	...	,,
Walton, Miss Annie	...	,,	,,	,,	...	,,
Walton, Miss Katharine	...	,,	,,	,,	...	,,
Waggott, Mrs. Margaret	...	,,	,,	,,	...	,,
Webster, Miss Margaret	...	,,	,,	,,	...	,,
Elliott, Miss Ethel	...	,,	,,	,,	...	,,
Goult, Miss Alice M.	.	,,	,,	,,	,,

Yorks.35/ VAD   Men's Detachment had 28 active members according to the North Riding War Report book. They met all wounded soldiers for Skelton and Saltburn hospitals and did escort duty for entertainments and orderly duties. Their Commandant was T.P. Gibson Esq. and the Medical Officer was Dr Burnett. During the latter part of 1918 the Detachment could not continue with their usual practices as many of the officers and members were actively engaged in other war·work.

Sleights Red Cross Auxiliary Hospital

"Sleights Red Cross Auxiliary Hospital," Sleights.

Building lent by ...	The Sleights Institute Committee.
Date of opening	24th November, 1914.
Date of closing	27th November, 1918.
No. of Beds	30.
Total number of patients treated ...	388.
No. of deaths	None.
Hospital affiliated to ...	East Leeds War Hospital.
Commandant	Miss S. B. Yeoman, O.B.E.
Assistant Commandant ...	... Miss Averil Stobart.
Medical Officer ... Dr. T. H. English, "Netherby," Sleights.
Matron ...	Mrs English, A.R.R.C. (Honorary).
Quartermaster	... Miss Averil Stobart.
Staffed by ...	Yorks./38 V.A.D., and Trained Nurses.

The original architect's drawing of Sleights Institute which was opened in 1908 and used as a reading room. The caretaker lived in the cellar. Now called Sleights Village Hall it hosts a wide range of community events and activities.

136

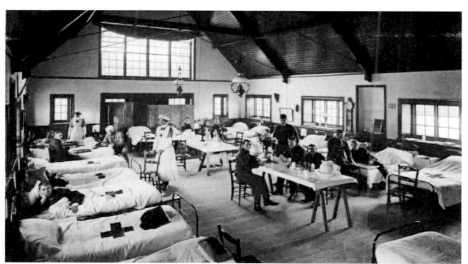

Yorks./38. Sleights.

Commandant   Miss Yeoman, O.B.E.
Medical Officer: Dr. Thos. English.
Quartermaster: Miss Stobart.

Name.	Record of War Service.	Part time or Whole time.
Yeoman, Miss Sophia Bruce ...	Sleights Hospital. Commandant ...	Whole time
Stobart, Miss Averil Culler ...	„ Quartermaster ...	„
Atkinson, Mrs. Mary ...	„ ...	„
Pickering, Miss Elsie ...	„ ...	Part time
Jackson, Miss Margaret ...	„ ...	„
Richardson, Miss Mabel ...	„ ...	„
Buckler, Mrs. Mary ...	„ ...	„
Sutcliffe, Miss Irene ...	„ ...	„
Earp, Miss Edith ...	„ ...	„
Rhodes, Mrs. Adelaide ...	„ ...	„
Brooks, Miss Mabel	„ ...	„
Clegg, Mrs. Clara ...	„ ...	„
Villers Brown, Miss Margaret ...	„ ...	„
Blantern, Miss Mary ...	„ ...	„
Blantern, Miss Elsie	„ ...	„
Boyle, Mrs. Lilian ...	„ ...	„
Floud, Mrs. Marion ...	„ ...	„
Clark, Mrs. Gertrude ...	„ ...	„
Williams, Miss Irene ...	„ ...	„
Welburn, Miss Lily ...	„ ...	„
Hutton, Miss Maria ...	„ ...	„
Gladstone, Miss Sibyl ...	„ ...	„
Dunwell, Miss Kate ...	„ ...	„
Manfield, Mrs. Mary ...	„ ...	„
Willshaw, Mrs. Elizabeth ...	„ ...	„
English, Miss Janet ...	„ ...	„
Weighill, Mrs. Marjorie ...	„ ...	„
Tuck, Miss Jane ...	„ ...	„
Myers, Mrs. Bessie ...	„ ...	„
English, Thos. ...	„ Doctor ...	„
English, Mrs. ...	„ Matron ...	„

Dr. Thomas Harks English
July 1916

Mrs Anna Louisa English
July 1916

Janet, the daughter of Dr and Mrs
English was a nurse at the hospital.

Miss Yeoman, the hospital Commandant.
Her two sisters were also nurses there.

It is reported in the Daily Gazette of Middlesbrough, 10th December 1914, that wounded soldiers at the hospital were treated to a motor ride to Scarborough by Miss C Yeoman, one of the sisters of the Commandant, and to dinner at the Grand Hotel by Dr English. On their return to Sleights they played a billiard handicap game at the Institute with valuable prizes being given. Councillor F G Horth addressed the men, congratulating them on their progress towards recovery and wishing them success. Bombadier Aymes responded on behalf of the men.

Story of a soldier
at Sleights

PRIVATE W. ROGERS.

1st Worcester Regiment, in a Yorkshire hospital; deaf and dumb from shock of bursting shell, but progressing satis-factorily. Son of Mr. and Mrs. G. Rogers, of Bredon, and one of four brothers now serving in the Army.

The next year it is reported on March 31st that a further batch of wounded soldiers arrived at Sleights Red Cross Hospital. The majority were suffering from bullet wounds received at Ypres and Neuve Chapelle. They were met at the station by Dr English and Red Cross officials and five severe cases were transported on stretchers by members of the Grosmont Ambulance Corps.

139

By a remarkable twist of fate, a Private in the Duke of Wellington's Regiment found that one of the nurses caring for him was the mother of a young officer under whom he had served and whom he saw killed.

Another soldier nursed at Sleights was Lt Corporal Lorains who is seen here as the goalkeeper in a football match before the war..

.. and then in a group photo in the hospital album.

Time for a cup of tea while playing cards? Keeping the wounded soldiers occupied was part of the job.

Doctor and Mrs English and other staff chat to the patients.

Dr. English, who wanted very much to serve his country, had been on the National Reserve since 1912; but, as he was aged forty-nine at the outbreak of WW1, there was little likelihood of him seeing active service; and so for him the starting and carrying on of an enterprise which, for a small village, turned out to be so remarkably successful, must have been very satisfying; and it seems likely that his energy and open-hearted eagerness in leading alongside Miss Yeoman such a scheme could never have been put to better use.

In addition, his wife's personal supervision of the nursing arrangements no doubt made for a unity of purpose among her staff which held them together, and brought out the best in each of the small band of keen and patriotic women who, with no previous experience, soon reached a high degree of skill.

The work not only included nursing but many jobs which now no longer exist, such as filling and cleaning four large hanging paraffin lamps which provided illumination for the ward, and twenty smaller bedside ones, every day; the cleaning of the centre ward table, set out with wash basins and jugs for the patients, and the carrying of water for the same, the nearest taps being down two flights of steps; and of course, the general cleaning of the ward itself, and a small room at the side used for surgery, all without the benefit of any electrical appliances.

Mrs. English attended every day for the morning shift, and again in the evening from six until nine receiving the night report from the Charge Nurse in the morning, and giving instructions for the night before she left in the evening. She also acted as masseuse when necessary, and on Sunday evenings gave the patients one of their greatest pleasures by accompanying them on the piano in their impromptu concerts and sing-songs.

The kitchen was also staffed by volunteers and, in addition, Girl Guides and Boy Scouts came regularly; the girls to peel potatoes and wash and polish ash trays, the boys to clean the shoes and run errands. Indeed, it would be true to say that almost everyone in the district was proud to help in any way they could.

141

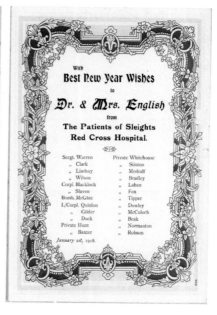

It was usual for patients to record their thanks for the care received but not all left gifts.

Sergeant A. Curtis, Royal Field Artillery.
Corporal L. Anthony, Lancashire Fusiliers.
Corporal W. C. Hennessey, 15th Hussars.
Bombardier A. E. Aymes, Royal Field Artillery.
Private W. Bird, Lincolnshire Regiment.
Private W. Woolley, Devonshire Regiment.
Private H. Fuller, Suffolk Regiment.
Private J. Duncanson, King's Own Scottish Borderers.
Private J. Stewart, Royal Inniskilling Fusiliers.
Private W. Rogers, Worcestershire Regiment.
Private A. Williams, Worcestershire Regiment.
Private A. A. Shaw, Black Watch.
Private B. Riley, Royal West Kents.
Private W. Channell, Dorset Regiment.
Private J. Machin, King's Own Yorks. Light Infantry.
Private N. Ehrenberg, Wiltshire Regiment.
Private J. Meneilly, Royal Irish Rifles.
Private A. Davis, Army Service Corps.
Private T. H. Jones, Monmouthshire Regiment.

Recognition from some more grateful patients. The names of the donors of this illuminated address were printed on the back.

Weston Auxiliary Military Hospital, Scarborough

"Weston Auxiliary Military Hospital,"
Westwood, Scarborough.

Date of opening	14th April, 1915.
Date of closing	27th August, 1915
No. of Beds	35.
Total number of patients treated ...	160.
No. of deaths	One.
Hospital affiliated to ...	Military Hospital, York.
Commandant The late Lt.-Colonel W. Hastings-Fowler, V.D.	
Medical Officers	Dr. C. E. Salter.
	Dr. Walter Griffin.
Staffed by	Yorks./66 and 80.

This is the only hospital that we have been unable to find, but it was open for such a short space of time that possibly it was only to cope with a large influx of soldiers at that particular time. We do know that one of the nurses from Scarborough, Edith Elizabeth Taylor, died in June 1917 from septic pneumonia as a result of nursing an infected patient. She was the daughter of the late John W Taylor who had previously been the Medical Officer of Health in Scarborough and sister in law of Dr. C.E Salter who was the medical officer of this hospital.

The Yorkshire Post of 8th June 1917 reports that she was buried with military honours and had been borne into church by wounded soldiers from the hospital. She has a memorial in the tryptich in St Martin on the Hill Church, Scarborough with nurse Alice Flintoff who was a member of the Territorial Nursing Service.

Several nurses died during the war in the North Riding who are commemorated in York Minster in beautifully illuminated cupboards, next to the Five Sisters Window. All women who died in war service during WW1 are named.

The names of the nurses are: Miss Eva Dorothy Yeoman Yorks /38 Sleights, Miss Gwen Richardson Yorks/42 Stokesley, Mrs Mary Peck Yorks/20 Saltburn, Miss Jane Morgan Yorks/34 Pickering, Miss Elizabeth Preston Yorks/24 Crathorne and Yarm, Miss Edith Taylor Yorks/66 Scarborough, Miss Jane Watnough Yorks/16 Constable Burton.

Also commemorated on these screens, in the cupboard for munitions workers, is Dolly Clarke from Slingsby in the North Riding who died in September 1916 of Toluol poisoning when she was 22 years old. Toluol formed toluolene which when nitrated with a mixture of sulphuric acid and nitric acid, after further nitration, produces TNT (Trinitrotoluene).

As Ursula Lascelles recorded in one of her scrapbooks "I managed to get Mrs Dolly Clarke's name put on the memorial screen and Mrs Lascelles and I took Mrs Hardy, her mother and little May Clarke, her daughter to the dedication,"

The dedication was to mark the restoration of the Five Sisters window to which Slingsby had contributed £1-4s-6d towards the estimated cost of £3000. The window was restored using lead found at Rievaulx Abbey and given to the Minster by Lord Feversham, particularly appropriate as Duncome Park had been a Red Cross hospital. The window was dedicated in 1925 at a service attended by the Duchess of York, later Queen Elizabeth, the Queen Mother.

The door here carries the statement attributed to Edith Cavell, one of the most famous nurses to die in the war, as she was shot by the German army for enabling soldiers to escape from capture.

Commandant and Medical Officer : **Dr** Chas. Salter.

Assistant Commandant :   Miss Shield

Name.		Record of War Service.		Part time or Whole time.
Blackburn, Miss Clara	..	3rd Mil. Hos., Westboro' ; Mil. Hos. Scarboro' ; Foxborough Hall Red Cross Hospital, Melton, Suffolk ; V.A.D Hos., The Great Hermitage, Higham, Rochester	..	Part & Whole
Blackburn, Miss Phoebe	..	Weston House, Scarboro', and the Great Hermitage, Higham, Rochester	..	Part & Whole
Bolton, Miss Hilda	..	3rd Mil. Hos., Westboro' ; Weston House Red Cross Hos., and Mil. Hos., Scarboro'	..	Part time
Catt, Mrs. Emily	..	3rd Mil. Hos., Westboro' ; Weston House Red Cross Hos., and Mil. Hos., Scarboro'	..	,,
Coombes, Miss Mariam	..	3rd Mil. Hos., Westboro', Scarboro' ; Queen Mary's Mil. Hos., Whalley, Manchester	..	Part & Whole
Cadman, Miss Ethel	..	Weston House, Scarboro' ; 1st War Hos., Rubery, Birmingham	..	,,
Flint, Miss Elsie	..	3rd Mil. Hos., Westboro' ; Weston House, Scarboro' ; and E. Selwyn College, Cambridge	..	,,
Godfrey, Miss Violet	..	3rd Mil. Hos., Westboro', Scarboro', and Malta Mil. Hos.	..	,,
Jepson, Miss Charlotte	..	Weston House Red Cross Hos. and Mil. Hos., Scarboro'	..	Part time
Muil, Miss Agnes	..	3rd Mil. Hos Westboro', Weston House, & Mil. Hos., Scarbro'	..	,,
Marche, Miss Gwynnette	..	Weston House and Mil. Hos., Scarboro' ; 2nd Northern Gen East Leeds War Hos., Leeds	..	Part & Whole
Maclean, Mrs. Jeanna	..	Weston House Red Cross Hos. and Mil. Hos., Scarboro'	..	Part time
Nicbolls, Miss Everild	..	Lady Evelyn Mason's Hospital, Bruton St., London	..	Whole time
Nicbolls, Miss Monica	..	Military Hospital, Wakefield	..	,,
Paton, Mrs. Edith	..	3rd Mil. Hos., Westboro' ; Weston House ; and The Mil. Hos., Scarbrough	..	Part time
Peirson, Mrs. Katherine	..	Weston House Red Cross Hos. and The Mil. Hos. Scarbrough	..	,,
Smith, Miss Muriel	..	3rd Mil. Hos., Westboro, Scarbrough, and the 3rd Western Gen Hos., Pendleton, Manchester	..	Part & Whole
Stephens, Miss Eleanor	..	3rd Mil. Hos., Westboro', Weston House and Mil. Hos. S'bro.	..	,,
Shield, Miss Beatrice	..		..	,,
Spencer, Miss Eva	..	Tooting Military Hospital	..	Whole time
Winder, Miss Dorothy	..	France	..	,,
Wabre, Miss Hermione	..	Weston House, Scarborough	..	,,
Waithman, Miss Isabel	..	Weston House and The Mil. Hos., Scarborough	..	Part time
Bastiman, Miss Maude	..	The Mil. Hos., Scarborough	..	,,
Copperthwaite, Mrs. Laura	..	,, ,,	..	,,
Clarke, Miss Lois	..	,, ,,	..	,,
Gaunt, Miss Clara	..	,, ,,	..	,,
Morton, Mrs. Flora	..	,, ,,	..	Whole time
Murray, Miss May Gawler	..	,, ,,	..	Part time
Taylor, Mrs. Jeanette (nee J. Fowler)	..	,, ,,	..	,,
Wray, Miss Catherine	..	,, ,,	..	,,
Woods, Miss Gertrude	..	,, ,,	..	,,
Wilson, Mrs. Alice	..	,, ,,	..	,,
Willan, Miss Jessica	..	,, ,,	..	,,
Bayes, Mrs. Janet	..	,, ,,	..	Whole time

The other little nugget of information about Scarborough is a notice about Boyes sale in November 1914 where it stated that there was £300 worth of wool in the sale which was " suitable for soldiers and sailors comforts".

Wharton Hall Hospital, Skelton

"Wharton Hall Hospital," Skelton-in-Cleveland.

Building lent by ...	Colonel W. H. A. Wharton, O.B.E.
Date of opening	1st April, 1915.
Date of closing	19th January, 1919.
No. of Beds	36.
Total number of patients treated ...	480.
No. of deaths	None.
Hospital affiliated to ...	East Leeds War Hospital.
Commandant	E. J. Burnett, Esq., M.D.
Hon. Commandant ...	Mrs. W. H. A. Wharton.
Medical Officer E. J. Burnett, Esq., M.D., Saltburn-by-the-Sea.	
Matron	Miss Private, A.R.R.C.
Quartermasters ...	Miss W. Wharton and Miss Heslop.
Staffed by	Yorks. 20.

"The Wharton Hall has been altered and been made into a most comfortable hospital. The people in the district have helped in fitting and by lending beds, bedding etc."

On 1st April 1915 the first 15 patients were admitted,12 of them directly from the Front. There is no doubt that the patients thoroughly enjoyed good care at the hospital as this report in the Daily Gazette from Middlesbrough for 19th April 1915 states "The wounded soldiers sent to Skelton are spending an enjoyable time at the Wharton Hall which, thanks to the alterations carried out by Colonel W.H.A Wharton is now a commodious hospital in the charge of the local Red Cross Society. Beds are provided for 15 men and the soldiers greatly appreciate the kindness shown to them."

Miss Private was appointed as Matron by Col. and Mrs. Wharton and trained nurses provided for night duty. Barbara Private who had been born in Malta, nursed at the North Riding Infirmary prior to becoming Matron. She was forty years old at the beginning of the War.

Nurses from Saltburn visited on the afternoons of Saturday and Wednesday.

Mrs Isabella French had been Matron of a convalescent home during the Boer War at 4 East Road Skelton which was also used during WW1 when Wharton Hall was overflowing with wounded soldiers. Her husband was Colonel Wharton's chauffeur.

Yorks./20.   Saltburn and Skelton.

Commandant : Dr. E. J. Burnett.
Hon. Commandant : Mrs. W. H. A. Wharton.
Medical Officer : Dr. E. J. Burnett.

Name.	Record of War Service.	Part time or Whole time.
Austin, Mrs. Mary	Skelton Red Cross Auxiliary Hospital	Part time
Bell, Mrs. Isabella	,,	,,
Brown, Miss Emily	Secretary (Skelton). Skelton Red Cross Auxiliary Hospital.	,,
Bulman, Miss Florence M.	Secretary (Saltburn) ,, ,, ,,	,,
Clark, Mrs. Alice	Skelton Red Cross Auxiliary Hospital	,,
Codman, Mrs. Bertha	,, ,, ,, . ,,	,,
Collier, Miss Hannah M.	,, ,, ,,	,,
Farrow, Miss Marie	,, ,, ,,	,,
French, Mrs. Isabella	,, ,, ,,	,,
Hamilton, Mrs. Maude	,, ,, ,,	,,
Heslop, Miss Ethel	Quartermaster. Skelton Red Cross Auxiliary Hospital.	,,
Lambert, Miss Margaret	Skelton Red Cross Auxiliary Hospital	,,
Littleboy, Mrs. Agnes	,, ,, ,, and Saltburn	,,
Mackenzie, Mrs. Isabella	,, ,, ,,	,,
McBain, Mrs. Margaret F.	,, ,, ,,	,,
MacNay, Mrs. Constance	,, ,, ,,	,,
Melliship, Mrs. Lyla	,, ,, ,,	,,
Moodie, Mrs. Mary E.	,, ,, ,,	,,
Parr, Miss Catherine	,, ,, ,,	,,
Pearson, Mrs. Emily	,, ,, ,,	,,
Pierson, Miss Margaret	Military Hospitals, France and Italy	Whole time
Rapp, Mrs. Lillian	Lady Superintendent. Skelton Red Cross Auxiliary Hospital..	Part time
Thorp, Miss Elizabeth	Skelton Red Cross Auxiliary Hospital	,,
Thubron, Miss Elizabeth	,, ,, ,,	,,
Toy, Miss Mabel	,, ,, ,,	,,
Toy, Miss Doris	,, ,, ,,	,,
Watts, Miss Winifred	,, ,, ,,	,,
Whatron, Miss W. M.	Quartermaster. Skelton Red Cross Auxiliary Hospital	,,
Williamson, Mrs. Lily	Skelton Red Cross Auxiliary Hospital	,,
Wilkinson, Miss Laura	,, ,, ,,	,,
Wright, Mrs.	,, ,, ,,	,,

Mrs. Beatrice Sibley, member of Yorks 4 detachment Loftus and Brotton, also served at Wharton Hall, as did Miss Dorothy Dixon, who acted as Secretary. Other members of Yorks 4 had wide and varied careers as V.A.D.s as can be seen from this service record sheet.

Miss Alethea Wood worked at 1st Northern General Hospital in Newcastle and then at a hospital in Calais from July 1916 to August 1919. She was mentioned in despatches.

Yorks/4. Loftus and Brotton.

Commandant and Medical Officer : Dr. H. Stonehouse.

Name.	Record of War Service.	Part time or Whole time.
Lynch-Blosse, Miss Theodora M.	New Zealand Hospital	Whole time
Colley, Miss H. Robina M. ...	Apr. to Oct., 1917, Mil. Hospital, Park Hall Camp, Oswestry ; Oct., 1917, to Apr., 1919. Citadel Mil. Hospital, Cairo, Egypt ; May—June, 1919. 3rd London Gen. Hos., Wandsworth ; Oct.—Dec., 1919, Mil. Hos., Park Hall Camp, Oswestry ; Dec., 1919 (to present time), Alexandra Hos., Cosham, Hants. ...	Whole time
Darnton, Miss Mabel ...	Leicester Base Hospital ...	,,
Errington, Miss Mary B. ...	June 30th, 1915, to June, 1916. 1st Northern Gen. Hospital, Newcastle-on-Tyne ; June 1916. to Mar. 27th, 1917, 10th Gen. Hos., Rouen, B.E.F., France ; April 17th, 1918, to Dec., 1919, The Lord Derby War Hospital, Warrington Assistant Nurse ...	,,
Stonehouse, Mrs. Jessie ...	Sister, V.A.D. Hospital, Sunnyside, Whalley Range, Manchester ...	,,
Sayer, Miss Jessie ...	Military Hospital, Lincoln ...	,,
Wood, Miss Alethea ...	May, 1915, to July, 1916, 1st Northern, Hos., Newcastle-on-Tyne ; July, 1916, to Aug., 1919, 30th Gen. Hos., Calais (Mentioned in Despatches) ; Aug. to Nov., 1919, 32nd Stationary, Hos., Wimereaux. Assistant Nurse ...	,,
Wood, Miss May Wilson ...	Skelton Hospital ...	Part time
Temple, Miss Sarah S. ...	1st Mar., 1917. to June 30th, 1917, Bethnal Green Hos. ; Nov., 1917, to June, 1918, 3rd Gen. Hos., France ; Aug. 1918, to present time, Ripon Military Hospital ...	Whole time
Slade (Née Jenkins), Mrs. Gwendolyn...	1st Northern Gen. Hos., Newcastle-on-Tyne ...	Whole time
Dixon, Miss Dorothy ...	Secretary, Skelton Hospital, and American R.C.H., London ...	Part time
Sibley, Mrs. Beatrice ...	Skelton Hospital ...	,,

Two men's Detachments were formed in 1915, Yorks.3 Skelton with 39 members under the Commandant T.Varty and with the Medical Officer Dr. R. Botham, and Yorks. 13 Brotton with 24 members and Dr. M. Caldwell as both Commandant and Medical Officer.

Members of Yorks 3 attended weekly practices until the end of 1918 and were responsible for bringing the wounded to the hospital. They were inspected by Maj. Gen. Sir W.G.A. Bedford K.C.B. and Maj R.L. Bower C.M.G., County Director, and they paraded when H.R.H. the Duke of Connaught visited Skelton in June 1918.

DONATIONS.		£	s.	d.
Dr. Stonehouse ...	...	1	0	0
Rev. and Miss Williamson	...	1	10	0
Mrs. Collins ...	...	1	0	0
Mrs. G. H. Anderson ...	...	1	1	0
Mr. Ashley ...	...	1	1	0
Dr. Stephen ...	...	1	0	0
Mrs. Lewis Newsham ...	...	1	0	0
T. E. Errington, Esq. ...	...		10	0
Mrs. Errington	...		10	0
Mrs. T. Harrison (Sen.) ...	...		10	0
Mrs. Stonehouse ...	...		7	8
Miss Cochrane... ...	...		5	0
Miss West ...	...		5	0
Miss Webster ...	...		15	0
Mrs. Stephen ...	...		5	0
Miss Farr ...	...		15	0
Miss Barton ...	...		5	0
Miss Ellis ...	...		5	0
Miss Errington	...		2	6
Mr. Ferguson ...	...		5	0
Dr. Stephen's children for matches ...		1	7
Staff Junior Council School (Loftus) ...		1	0	0
,, Infants' ,, ,, ,, ...		1	1	0
Anon. ...	...		4	6
Loftus Tradesmen's Reform Club ...		1	13	0
Mrs. Pybus (Easington) ...	...		2	6
		£16	14	9

STATEMENT OF INCOME AND EXPENDITURE.

INCOME.	£	s.	d.	EXPENDITURE.	£	s.	d.
Donations	16	14	9	Materials purchased ; made into Gar-			
Other Income, viz. :—				ments (sent to Headquarters) ...	11	2	10
1914, Sept., Parish Church Collection	4	7	4	Cheque Book		1	0
,, Mothers' Union, per Mrs.				Wool	2	9	6
Ramsden		16	0	Expenses of Lecture		14	6
Oct., Lecture by Dr. and Mrs. Stain-				Sent to Belgian Relief Fund	12	15	0
thorpe	13	9	6	Expenses of Concert	1	18	2
1915, March, Concert (Staithes Pierettes)	11	8	6	,, Garden Party ...	1	18	6
June, Garden Party (Hall Grounds) ...	33	1	5	Calico for Bandages		11	5
Aug., Church and Street Collections ...	5	4	6	Expenses of Sale		10	6
Sept., Sale of Flowers, etc.	26	17	9	May, Oxo and Swiss Milk to France	3	9	4
,, Collected by Mrs. Carter ...	1	2	8	July, Parcels of Comforts to Front ...	5	11	2½
,, Harvest Collections Liverton Church	5	5	4	Aug., ,, ,, ,, ...	7	16	11½
Oct., Sale of Flags	1	2	6	Sent to Headquarters	1	2	6
Nov., Collected by Mrs. Carter		8	0	Sept., Parcels to Soldiers at Front ...	8	12	4
Dec., Concert (and Subs. to same),				Oct., ,, ,, ,,	11	16	5
Loftus Members at Loftus ...	17	10	10	Nov., ,, ,, ,,	13	7	8
Bank Interest		3	3	Expenses of Concert	1	10	10
				Total Expenditure	85	8	8
				Balance in Bank	52	3	8
	£137	12	4		£137	12	4

Certified correct this 6th day of March, 1916.   Mrs. WHARTON,
    W. A. STEPHEN, Auditor.   District Representative.

1 Women's Detachment	YORKS.	STRENGTH	p.p. Dr. H. Stonehouse, Commandant,
(Loftus and Brotton).	4	40	W. A. Stephen, M.D.

Fundraising took place with sales of flowers, a concert by Staithes Pierettes, a garden party in the Hall grounds. Sales of flags and street collections raised £137- 12s- 4d in 1915 which was used to buy material to make garments to be sent to Headquarters, wool for knitting comforts, and calico for bandages.

£12-15s- 0d was sent to the Belgian Relief Fund, as well as monthly parcels of comforts to the soldiers at the Front, which included Oxo and Swiss Milk.

In September 1915 the Cleveland Miners Association decided to send a Christmas parcel to every man serving with the armed forces at the Front "not to exceed 8 shillings". The workmen's contribution to the war relief fund for the next three months was devoted to this purpose.

80 parcels were sent off, each parcel containing: 1 muffler, 1 pair of socks, 1 pair of mittens, 1 towel, 2 handkerchiefs, 1 pair laces, card of buttons, packet of notepaper, 1 packet of Cocoa, 3 tubes of Pine Tablets, 4 packets of cigarettes or 1oz. of tobacco, a tin of Vaseline, and a calico bag.

A Soldier's Story
A cook at a big house in Skelton became friendly with one of the wounded soldiers, Private John Henry Shambly, and invited him back to her house for tea. There he fell in love with her daughter, and, after the war, came back to Skelton to marry her.

The Daily Gazette for Middlesbrough on 19th of June 1918 reported on a royal visit to Skelton in Cleveland:

COMPLIMENT TO SKELTON

The people of Skelton in Cleveland today had an unexpected compliment paid to their village as thanks to a suggestion from Mrs Wharton, the Duke of Connaught consented to include it in the list of places visited by him today.

His Royal Highness motored from Kirkleatham on his way to Guisborough and was received with rousing cheers from nearly a thousand children who lined the road from the Red Cross Hospital to the village Green.

In front of the old soldiers home, which during the Boer War and some years afterwards Col Wharton had maintained for convalescent soldiers, and which is now used as an annexe of the Wharton Red Cross Hospital, there were drawn up wounded soldiers and nurses from both Cliftden and Skelton Hospitals. As well as representatives of the Red Cross detachment and other Societies, the Duke was received by Col and Mrs Wharton, who afterwards presented Miss Wharton (one of the Quartermasters at the hospital), the Rector (Reverend H M Drake) and Mr T Varty JP (Manager of Skelton Park Pit)

The Duke spoke to the wounded soldiers and local men who were no longer able to serve due to "lost limbs and wounds".

The report also mentioned that the Duke spent time talking to the children lining the route, and before leaving he signed his name in the Red Cross Hospital visitors book.

Manor House Hospital, Stokesley

" The Manor House Hospital," Stokesley.

Building lent by	Mrs. Gjers, o.b.e.
Date of opening	October 28th, 1914.
Date of closing	January 18th, 1919.
No. of Beds	60.
Total number of patients treated ...	801.
No. of deaths	None.
Hospital affiliated to	East Leeds War Hospital.
Commandant	Mrs. L. J. Gjers, o.b.e.
Medical Officers	Wm. Yeoman, Esq., M.B.
	Harold Walker, Esq., F.R.C.S.
Matron	Miss Jeffrey.
Quartermaster	Miss Clara Barker.
Staffed by	Yorks./42.

The Manor House in Stokesley could originally be dated back to 1066 but at the time of the war the remaining features were all Victorian. During the 19th Century it belonged to the Hildyards who were responsible for building Stokesley Town Hall and then it was owned by the Wynne Finch family. Mr Wynne Finch died in 1914 and the family lived in Busby Hall while the house was used as a hospital during the war. The Gjers family who ran the hospital eventually bought the house in 1919. During WW2 troops were billeted there as it was empty. At one time it became the offices for Stokesley Rural District Council and at the time of writing is up for sale again.

Soldiers with nursing staff and Dr Yeoman outside the hospital

Yorks./42. Stokesley.

Commandant : Mrs. Gjers, O.B.E.
Medical Officer : Dr. W. Yeoman.

Name.	Record of War Service.	Part time or Whole time.
Gjers, Mrs. Annie G.	Commandant. Auxiliary Military Hospital, Stokesley	Whole time
Yeoman, Dr. William	P.M.O. ,, ,, ,,	Part time
Walker, Dr. Harold	Surgeon. ,, ,, ,,	,,
Jeffrey, Miss Jane	Aux. Mil. Hospital, Stokesley	Whole time
Barker, Miss Clara	Quartermaster. Aux. Mil. Hospital, Stokesley	,,
Forbes, Miss Nina	Deputy Quartermaster. Aux. Mil. Hospital, Stokesley	Part time
Auton, Miss Emma	Aux. Mil. Hospital, Stokesley	Whole time
Armstrong, Mrs. Dorothy	,, ,,	Part time
Briggs, Miss Margaret	,, ,,	,,
Barker, Miss Elizabeth	,, ,,	,,
Dobson, Miss Sybil O.	,, ,,	,,
Gjers, Miss Olga G.	,, ,,	,,
Goldsbrough, Miss Louise	,, ,,	,,
Grant, Miss Agnes	,, ,,	,,
Harkess, Miss E. Mary	,, ,,	,,
Ingledew, Mrs. Mary E.	,, ,,	,,
Kyle, Miss Susan G. L.	,, ,,	,,
Lynch, Miss Rose	,, ,,	,,
Littlefair, Mrs. Marion	,, ,,	,,
Leng, Miss Margaret	,, ,,	,,
Mitchison, Miss Annie	,, ,,	,,
Morgan, Miss Sarah E.	,, ,,	,,
Nelson, Miss Evelyn M.	,, ,,	,,
Richardson, Mrs. Emily H.	,, ,,	,,
Edwards, Mrs. Nora H.	,, ,,	,,
Robinson, Miss Nellie	,, ,,	,,
Herring, Mrs. Jane A.	,, ,,	,,
Shilbeck, Miss Ruth	,, ,,	,,
Swainson, Mrs. Charlotte	,, ,,	,,
Walker, Miss Eva	,, ,,	,,
Wright, Miss Elizabeth	,, ,,	,,
Yeoman, Miss Irene	,, ,,	Whole time
Chapman, Miss Elsie	,, ,,	Part time
Kyle, Miss Frances L.	,, ,,	,,
Musgrave, Miss Gladys	,, ,,	,,
Norman, Miss Madge	,, ,,	,,
Hall, Mrs. Gwen	,, ,,	,,
Sidgwick, Miss Muriel	,, ,,	,,
Wrightson, Miss Elizabeth	,, ,,	,,
Wrightson, Miss Dorothy	,, ,,	,,
Wilkinson, Miss Clara	,, ,,	,,

Back row:
Miss Eva Walker, Jane Sayers, Mary Mudd (grand-daughter of Chas Farrow — see below), Dorothy Maynard, Miss Morgan, Miss Eliz. Wright, Miss Swainson, Miss Isabel Jones, Miss Clara Briggs (Cook at Busby Hall)
Third Row:
Miss Auton, Susie Kyle, Evie Nelson, Agnes Grant, Mr Harris (Carlton schoolmaster), Gladys Musgrave, Mr Littlefair, Mrs Christie, Mr Ed. Knight, Rose Lynch, Mary Holborn, Miss Helen Wynne-Finch (family owned the Manor House)
Second row:
Mrs Kyle, Mr Chas Farrow (Stokesley Draper), Miss Nina Forbes (whose two brothers were both killed in the War), Sister Grainge (Qualified SRN), Mrs Anne Gjers (Commandant), Dr Yeoman (Chairman of the Stokesley Health Board), Miss Clara Barker, Mr Ted Marley, Miss Mills (of the Tees shipbuilders Gjers Mills & co)
Front row:
Miss Louise Goldsborough, Miss Margaret Leng, Mrs Littlefair, Miss Olga Gjers (daughter of Anne and later wife of Commander Gloag, Miss Irene Yeoman (doctor's daughter), Miss Mary Harkess (daughter to another Tees shipbuilding family), Miss Phyllis Raby, the Richardson sisters Gwen and Norma, Miss Sybil Dobson

Names and notes of V.A.D.s and other Hospital Volunteers in the photograph donated to Stokesley Library in 1981 by Mrs Sherrett, niece of Miss Goldsborough.

AUTON Miss, V.A.D. - Farmer's daughter from Seamer. Father, John Auton of Harker Hill. Seamer, (244 acres). Living in Stokesley aged 90+ in 1982.
BARKER Miss - Oara, British Red Cross Society, Quartermaster. Father Allan Barker, Jeweller, cycle and motor dealer, North Yorks agent for RCH cars. Jeweller's shop later became Helms' shoe shop.
BRIGGS Mrs, V.A.D. - Cook at Busby Hall
CHRISTIE Mrs, V.A.D.
DOBSON Miss Sybil, V.A.D. - Kirby Grange. Father was Tom Dobson a landowner. He did not pass health test for Army so was Recruiting Officer in World War 1. The Dobson family planted trees in Kirby Churchyard to commemorate the Battle of

Waterloo - 1815. The side chapel windows in St Augustine's Lady Chapel are in memory of the Dobson family. Miss Sybil Dobson and her two sisters all served in both 1st and 2nd World Wars.

FORBES Miss Nina, V.A.D. - Father, William Guthrie Forbes, C.M., M.B. - died young. Mother lived at Springfield Villas. Both brothers killed in the war.

GJERS Mrs Ann Gatenby, OBE,- JP, Matron, Commandant of the Red Cross Hospitsl Widow of John Gjers of Gjers Mills and Co., Ship Owners at Middlesbrough Docks. She lived at Busby Hall and encouraged her staff to work at the Hospital. In 1920 she purchased and lived in the Manor House.

GJERS Miss Olga, V.A.D. - Daughter of the Matron. Married Ernest Richardson Gloag a captain in the Royal Navy. Two of her sons farmed outside Stokesley

GOLDSBOROUGH Miss Louie, V.A.D - A music teacher who lived on West Green, Stokesley. Her niece Mrs Sherrett donated the picture which hangs on the wall in Stokesley Library. Father, Thomas Goldsborough was Registrar of Births Deaths and Marriages for Stokesley and Relieving Officer for the Union.

GRAINGER Rachel, Sister. - Qualified S.RN. Born 1887, daughter of a West Hartlepool Mayor. Married 1919 to John Foster Ellerby, a Bank Manager at Eston.

GRANT Miss Aggie, V.A.D. - Married a soldier named Buckton of Swainby

HARKESS Miss Mary, V.A.D. - Her father, William Harkess was Mayor of Middlesbrough in 1911 when the Transporter Bridge was opened. They lived at Levenside House, Stokesley.

HARRIS Mr Sidney Howell - Elementary School Master from Carlton in Cleveland. Guard and Night Duty.

HOLBORN Miss Mary, V. A.D. - Her father was a Methodist Minister on the Stokesley Circuit.

INGLEDEW Mrs, V.A.D. - She was a children's nurse at Busby Hall.

JONES Miss Isobel, V.A.D. - Lived at West Green, Stokesley. Nursed invalid mother for years. Father was a Banker.

KNIGHT Mr. Ted. - Ambulance driver.

KYLE Mrs, V.A.D. - Nee Horsfall ofPotto Hall. Wife of Canon Kyle of Carlton in Cleveland, vicar of St. Botolph's Church.

KYLE Miss Susie, V.A.D. - The eldest daughter of Canon Kyle of Carlton in Cleveland. Married Mr. Pattison.

LENG Miss Maggie, V.A.D. - Family owned the village shop in Carlton in Cleveland, run by mother Mrs Elizabeth Leng. Father John Leng was a grocer and draper.

LITTLEFAIR Mrs, V.A.D. - Of Carlton in Cleveland. Children's nurse at Busby Hall.

LITTLEFAIR Mr. - Guard and Night Duty. Stretcher Bearer. Gamekeeper at Busby Hall.

LYNCH Miss Rose, V.A.D - Maid at Busby Hall.

MARLEY Mr. Ted - Chauffeur at Busby Hall and also for the Hospital.

MAYNARD Miss Dorothy, V.A.D. - Father William Maynard formerly farmer at Howe Hill Farm Ingleby Greenhow. Married Fred Armstrong of Stokesley. Brother Francis Algernon Maynard farmer ofHowe Hill Farm until1916.

MILLS Miss, V.A.D. - Gjers Mills &Co. Ship Builders and owners at Middlesbrough Docks.

MORGAN Miss, V.A.D. - Maid at Busby HalL

MUDD Miss May, V.A.D. - Father owned a china shop in what was later Farrows and Kitchings. Married W. MaskelL

MUSGRAVE Miss Gladys, V.A.D. - From Carlton in Cleveland. Married Mr Pennock and moved to Surrey.

NELSON Miss Evie, V.A.D. - Married Mr Metcalfe of Swainby.

RABY Miss Phyllis, V.A.D. - Of Carlton in Cleveland. Father John Raby, Farmer? Married Rodney Armstrong, grocer of Stokesley, of Henry Armstrong & Sons?

RICHARDSON, Misses Gwen & Norma, V.A.D.s - Father Edwin B. Richardson D.L. J.P., was a landowner who lived at Potto Hall which was later turned into a convalescent hospital and later still a Hotel. Gwen caught pneumonia and died while nursing.

SAYERS Miss Jane, V.A.D. - Married a soldier named Bob Heron.

SWAINSON Mrs, V.A.D. - Helped the village sick.

WALKER Miss Eva, V.A.D. - Had 2 brothers who were doctors in Middlesbrough.

WRIGHT Miss Lizzie, V.A.D. - An assistant teacher at Carlton School.

WRIGHTSON Miss Dorothy. - Along with her sister Elizabeth was born and lived at Ladycross Farm, Sexhow, which was part of the Skutterskelf Estate. Dorothy spent two years with her sister who was married to a tea planter in Darjeeling. She died at the age of 104 years.

WYNNE-FINCH Miss Helen, Daughter of Edward Heneage Wynne-Finch and Emily Caroline Marwood. Lived at Stokesley Manor House. Moved to her uncle's at Busby Hall with her mother when her father died in 1914. Mr George Marwood was her mother's brother.

YEOMAN Miss Irene, V.A.D. - Daughter of Dr. Yeoman. Married young and moved South.

A Nurse's Story

Nurse Rachel Crosby Grainger was born in Hartlepool in 1887. Her father, Barton Grainger was born in Robin Hood's Bay but moved to West Hartlepool when he was four. Barton was a quite well known character in Hartlepool. He was a butcher by trade but also involved in property buying and politics. He was on Hartlepool's first town council. Rachel was the only trained nurse at the hospital.

In 1918 Rachel married John Foster Ellerby, born in 1875 at Nunthorpe. He was named after his father and in 1911 was living in Brook House Stokesley with his widowed mother. He was "a bank clerk in charge". At the outbreak of war John was 38 and by the time of conscription 40. There is a John F Ellerby in the medal index for WW1 who received the British and Victory medals but it is not proved that this is John Foster Ellerby. However, working at the bank in Stokesley, he probably met Rachel whilst she was working at the VAD hospital. They married as soon as the war ended.

They had at least 2 children: Margaret J Ellerby born 1919 and John Foster Ellerby born 1926. Rachel herself died in 1971, whilst her husband had died in 1953. On her marriage of course she would have had to give up nursing. John Ellerby, her son, remembers his mother telling him that the convalescent soldiers would be taken out to Kildale Hall (home of the Turtons), Busby Hall (home of the Marwoods), and Potto Hall (home of the Richardsons) for afternoon tea.

One such outing to Potto Hall took place at Christmas 1916 where the soldiers enjoyed an excellent tea and entertainment provided by the Misses Richardson and friends with 2 amusing sketches, songs, pianoforte selection and duets.

Anne Gwendoline Richardson, one of the daughters from Potto Hall and niece of the Kitchings of Ayton Firs, was a VAD nurse at the hospital who was on duty on Christmas Day but then fell ill with pneumonia. Her death is recorded in the Middlesbrough Daily Gazette on January 8th 1918 where it states that the wounded soldiers of the hospital sent a floral tribute. Her name is included in the commemoration to all women who died on war service in York Minster.

In June 1915 the Men's Detachment, Yorks 19 was mobilised with 38 men and their Commandant Mr. L.F. Gjers, who was reported to have died in 1918. The men acted as night orderlies at the hospital throughout the war, although by 1918 their number had been reduced to only four.

Dr. William Metcalf Yeoman M.B. M.R.C.S. L.S.A. was born in Osmotherley and graduated from Newcastle and London Hospital Medical Schools. As well as being the Medical officer to the Manor House Hospital he served as the Medical Officer to the District Poor Law Institution and as the Certifying Factory Surgeon Stokesley District. He went on to be instrumental in introducing District Nurses to the area, and to promoting vaccination against smallpox, diphtheria, and scarlet fever, improving public health, particularly of babies and children.

Mrs. Yeoman organised the workparty in the area and Mrs. Gjers became the District Representative, as well as organising the local "Our Day" collections. In the summer of 1916 Mr. and Mrs. Gjers arranged an open air concert in the the grounds of the Manor House. Foreman and workmen of Gjers Mills (Ayresome Ironworks) were invited and a brake load attended. There and then the workers decided they needed to do something to help their wounded comrades, and on return to the works every man agreed to have at least a penny halfpenny a week stopped from their wage which raised £458- 15s- 4d from August 1916 to April 1919. Inside staff contributed £92 – 1s- 8d and the firm doubled these amounts to pay a monthly quota.

It was voted to pay 2/6 per week to each man in hospital which increased to 5/- as the cost of living rose. 10/- per week was paid to men convalescing at home.

£300 was distributed in the first 3 years among 53 men and 100 letters of good cheer sent to men in hospital. The widows were not forgotten, receiving 5/- per week with an extra 1/- for each child under 16.

Wounded Canadian soldiers and Red Cross nurses outside the Manor House.

The Manor House Hospital was well known, even in France, where wounded soldiers were told to "try to get to the hospital in Stokesley, North Yorkshire where it was brilliant."

The Red Cross service cards for Annie and Olga Gjers.

Stanwick Park Red Cross Hospital, Darlington

Mrs Wilson had the unfortunate experience of having to remove her Hospital three times. In December 1914 she established a Hospital at Croft Hall and in May 1915 was obliged to remove to Newton Morrell which was lent by the late Capt. Rowlandson. After his death in action at the end of 1916 the property was sold, and the Hospital was again moved to Stanwick Park. Unfortunately this property was required in August, 1918 and after an arduous, but fruitless, search for another suitable house Miss Wilson was obliged to close down her Hospital. After four and a half years continuous service Miss Wilson and several of her members volunteered and served first in a London Hospital and later in France.

Yorks/6. Barnard Castle.

Commandant : Miss Bell-Irving.
Lady Superintendent : Miss K. Emmerson, A.R.R.C.

Name.	Record of War Service.	Part time or Whole time
Bell-Irving, Miss Eva Margaretta	Stanwick Hos,, 1917 ; Viscountess Maitland's Aux. Hos., Thurlestone Castle, 1918 ; R.F.C. Hospital, 82 Eaton Square, London, Oct. to Dec., 1198	Part time
Emmerson, Miss (Nurse)	Lady Superintendent. Lent for War to Mrs. Claude Pease's Hospital	Part time
Maitland, Mrs. Ethel Mary	Quartermaster at Thurlestone Castle Hospital, 1918 ; and at Pembroke Lodge Hospital, South Kensington, London	,,
Alderson, Miss M. E.	Richmond Red Cross Hospital, Yorks., then at 2/1st S. Gen. Hospital, Birmingham ; served from 1917 till Aug., 1919	Whole time
Cruickshanks, Miss Jane	Thurlestone Castle Hospital, Berwickshire, 1918	Whole time
Gough, Miss Elsie	Stanwick Hospital, Yorks/36, 1917—18	Part time
Kinrush, Miss Katherine	Thurlestone Castle Aux. Hos., Jan. to Aug., 1918	,,
Milne, Miss Nellie (now invalided in Hospital, Elgin)	Served from June 1st, 1917, till April, 1919 ; invalided out at War Hospital, Stoke-on-Trent	Whole time
Shephard, Miss Florence	29 Stationary Hospital, Italian Ex. Force ; entered September, 1917	,,
Todd, Miss Margaret	County Hospital, York, for 15 months	,,
Percy, Miss Vera Noreen	Thurlestone Castle Aug. Hos , Berwickshire, 1918	,,
Ward, Miss Annie	Munition Worker during War)	,,

Station Pierce Bridge
Darlington R.X. Auy. H. Sh.E.R. Mrs Wilson
Stanwick Park Beds #082

Bradley Eliz E. J.C.	11.4.17	1.6.18	
Baker Louisa J.C.	1.6.18	23.8.18	
Wyer Madeline b J C	1.6.18	1.8.18	

Swinton Grange Red Cross Hospital, Malton

The Red Cross Hospital, Swinton Grange, Malton.

Building lent by	Major Clive Behrens, J.P.
Date of opening	September, 1914.
Date of closing	January, 1919.
No. of Beds	30.
Total number of patients treated ...	652.
No. of deaths	None.
Hospital affiliated to ...	East Leeds War Hospital.
Commandant	The Hon. Mrs. C. Behrens.
Medical Officers	Dr. Cecil Walker.
	Dr. de Merillonde.
	Dr. D. McCormick.
	Mr. Rhodes (dentist).
Matron	Miss Lucy Crowther.
Quartermaster	Miss Rose Peach.
Staffed by ...	Yorks./46 and 23 and Trained Nurses.

This splendid Hospital was established, organised and maintained entirely by Major and the Hon. Mrs. Clive Behrens.

Original architect's drawings of the house.

Swinton Grange was built by Lord Rothschild as a wedding gift for his daughter on her marriage to Clive Behrens in 1899. The gardens at one time contained mature examples of every known English species of tree. The property remained in the family until 1978 and then was used as office accommodation until the present time.

Charlotte Louisa Adela Evelina Behrens (1873 – 1947) was the daughter of the 1st Baron Rothschild who was a British banker and politician. She married Major Clive Behrens, a Yorkshire landowner, J.P. and Deputy Lieutenant.

Yorks./46. Swinton.

Commandant: The Hon. Mrs. C. Behrens.
Medical Officer: Dr. D. C. McCormick.

Name.	Record of War Service.		Whole time or Part time
Alexander, Miss Violet I	Swinton Grange Aux. Hospital, Oct. 1914 to 1919	...	Part time
Behrens, The Hon. Mrs. Clive			Whole time
	Commandant. ,, ,, ,,		
Behrens, Miss Peggy	Swinton Grange Aux. Hospital, Jan. 1918—1919	...	Part time
Banks, Mrs. Elizabeth	,, ,, Oct. 1914—1919	...	,,
Bradshaw, Miss Annie	,, ,, ,,	...	,,
Carter, Miss Catherine E.	,, ,, ,,	...	,,
Crosier, Mrs. Agnes	,, ,, ,,	...	,,
Calvert, Miss Evelyn	,, ,, ,,	...	,,
Denby, Miss Winifred	,, ,, Oct. 1914—1915 ; No. 4 Gen. Hos. B.E.F., 1916—1919 }	...	Whole time
Glynn, Mrs. Lilian	Swinton Grange Aux. Hospital, Oct. 1914—1919	...	Part time
Hickson, Mrs. Rose	,, ,, ,,	...	,,
Hudson. Miss Edith	,, ,, ,,	...	,,
Johnstone. Miss Kate	,, ,, ,,	...	,,
Lascelles, Mrs. Elizabeth M.	,, ,, ,,	...	,,
Lascelles, Miss Ursula	,, ,, Oct. 1914—1917 ; No. 6 General Hospital, 1917—1919 }	...	Whole time
Marriott, Miss Alice	Swinton Grange Aux. Hospital, Oct. 1914—1919	...	Part time
Martin, Miss Annie	,, ,, ,,	...	,,
Peach. Miss Rose	,, ,, ,,	...	,,
Peach, Miss Georgina	,, ,, ,,	...	,,
Porter, Miss Sarah	,, ,, ,,	...	,,
Romanes, Mrs. Cecily	,, ,, Jan. 1916—1919	...	,,
Shepherd. Mrs. Mary Ann E.	,, ,, Oct. 1914—1919	...	,,
Stuart, Miss Ada	,, ,, Oct. 1918—1919	...	,,
Strickland. Miss Laura	,, ,, 1917—1919	...	,,
Ward. Mrs. Margaret P.	,, ,, Oct. 1914—1919	...	,,
Wentworth. Miss Gladys	,, ,, Oct. 1914—1915; 2/1 So. Gen. Hospital, 1915—1916 ; 4 So. Gen. Hospital, 1916—1917 }	...	Whole time

Mrs Lascelles and Miss Alexander at Foxglove Cottage, the nurses' home, Swinton Grange Auxiliary Military Hospital.

TELEPHONE—MALTON 53.

BRITISH ✚ SOCIETY.

V.A.D. YORKS/46.

HEADQUARTERS	SWINTON GRANGE.		COMMANDANT—
POSTAL	MALTON.		THE HON MRS CLIVE BEHRENS.
TELEGRAMS	YORKS.		

December 30th, 1915.

Dear Mrs Lascelles,

We expect to get patients
to-day. Will you therefore please arrange for
Miss Hudson and Miss Calvert to come on duty .

I shall expect Miss Hudson on Saturday evening
but it will be quite in order if Miss Calvert only
gets here on Monday.

Yours very truly,

[signature]

MILITARY AUXILIARY HOSPITAL,
SWINTON GRANGE, MALTON, YORKS.

BRITISH ✚ SOCIETY.

TELEPHONE—MALTON 53
STATION—MALTON.

V.A.D YORKS 46.
COMMANDANT—
MRS. CLIVE BEHRENS

May 4th, 1915.

Dear Mrs Lascelles,

I hear from Leeds that I am
not getting any patients this week so I shall only
require one V.A.D.

I would be very glad to put Miss Alexander
up in the house, and, in that case, should not require
Miss Wentworth, but Peggy has been exposed to
infection from German Measles and the period of in-
cubation is not up till May 1 th. now, seeing that she
only had the other variety so short a time since, I
think it very unlikely that she will produce the
disease, but still it should be laid before Miss
Alexander in case she does not care to come.

Believe me,

Yours very truly,

[signature]

Mrs. Lascelles from Slingsby was a very active member in the running of the hospital. Trained nurses were also employed.

163

The appreciation of the soldiers is well recorded in the many letters kept by Ursula Lascelles, who was a V.A.D. at Swinton before going to Rouen No.6 General Hospital. Great efforts were made by the staff to entertain their patients, especially at Christmas. In December 1917 in addition to the usual Christmas festivities the patients, Sisters and nurses who were on duty went up to Swinton Grange House to be guests of Captain and Mrs. Behrens. The Medical Officer and a small house party were the only other guests present. Tea was followed by games, music and singing.

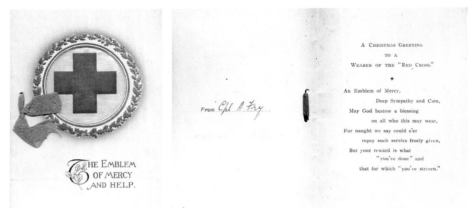

THE EMBLEM OF MERCY AND HELP.

A CHRISTMAS GREETING
TO A
WEARER OF THE "RED CROSS."
+
An Emblem of Mercy,
Deep Sympathy and Care,
May God bestow a blessing
on all who this may wear,
For naught we say could e'er
repay such service freely given,
But your reward is what
"you've done" and
that for which "you've striven."

From *Cpl A Fry*

The Commandant of the Yorks/23 Men's Detachment was Captain Clive Behrens. The Swinton Grange section of the Detachment all served as orderlies in the hospital, mostly on night duty, and were all on anti-aircraft work.

The financial report of 1915 shows interesting expenditure on the conversion of a motor car to an ambulance.

EXPENDITURE.	£	s.	d.
Expenses of Meetings, Lectures, &c.	8	3	8
Administration Expenses, including Printing, Stationery, Postage, Telegrams and Sundries ...	4	7	4
Other Expenditure, viz. :—			
Smithson & B's. A/c for 1st Aid Books	1	2	0
Suddaby's 1914 A/c	4	2	8
Piercy' A/c for Splints ...		7	6
Smithson & B's. A/c for 1st Aid Books		8	6
Hobson's & Son's A/c for Haversack	2	8	0
Subscription to Red Cross Hospital, Malton	30	0	0
Mennell's A/c for belts ...	3	0	0
Robson's A/c for lock, keys, &c.	1	7	0
Eddon's A/c for painting ...		8	0
Robson's A/c for Motor Car (to be converted into an Ambulance)	70	0	0
British Red Cross Society for flags	1	13	6
Yates' A/c for Canvas for Motor	1	17	0
Robson's A/c for brass buttons for Motor		13	6
Laverick's A/c for equipment ...	12	15	2
Total Expenditure	142	13	10
Balance in hand		5	0
Balance in Bank .. 29 18 0			
Less outstanding cheques 7 15 6			
	22	2	6
	£165	1	4

CAPT. CLIVE BEHRENS,
District Representative.

Dear Miss Lascelles

I wonder if you have forgotten me. I most certainly have not forgotten you, nor ever shall – but shall always remember your sympathy, gentleness and care, when I was in dear old Nº 6 General. What a bother I must have been to you and what labour and work during those hot hot days must I not have caused you? And yet you never seemed to mind or to tire in all your goodness to me. You will be pleased to hear that, altho' still in Hospital, I am practically well again – in fact I cant think why the M.O's seem so determined to keep me in dock. However I hope to get to France again in the Spring and strike one more blow for freedom. I do

hope you are keeping well and getting as much happiness as possible out of life. I trust also that your Mother and your Brother keep well. Will you please convey my kindest remembrances and grateful thanks to your friend, the young lady who occasionally acted for you, and who so thoughtfully provided me with coffee on several occasions. I have forgotten her name (my memory is so bad) and only remember that she was very bright and pretty and she told me her relatives lived in India or somewhere east of Suez.
Every good wish for your continued health and prosperity – From Your old sincere patient A. Fry

Ursula Lascelles

The Story of a VAD nurse.

Ursula Lascelles (born 9/7/1890 died 18/9/1992) lived in Sheriff-Hutton with her parents John, the Vicar in the village, and his wife Elizabeth who was 18 years his junior, together with her brother Lionel.

When John died in 1905 following a collapse in the pulpit while delivering a sermon on the subject of dying, Mrs Lascelles took the family to live with her father-in-law who was the local doctor in Slingsby, near Malton.

Ursula was educated in York at the Girls Grammar School, followed by three years at Wycombe Abbey in Buckinghamshire and then for a period of time in France.

At the outbreak of the First World War Ursula and her mother joined as VADs in the Yorks./46 Detachment based at The British Red Cross Hospital in Swinton Grange near Malton. Mrs Lascelles proved to be a driving force, not only in the hospital, but also as an active contributor to the local community war efforts. Her work fundraising, making and collecting comforts for the troops, and inspiring others is well recorded in letters and other documents in the archives held by the North Yorkshire County Council Records Office in Northallerton.

Ursula worked at the hospital as a VAD from 1914 to 1917 but was determined to nurse in France where she felt she could be more useful.

Many letters survive between herself and Dame Katharine Furse who was the head of the Joint Women's VAD department at Devonshire House in London, pleading her case to be sent to serve in France. Eventually with some support from the Hon. Mrs Behrens the Commandant at Swinton Grange, Ursula was accepted to work at the No.6 General Hospital in Rouen where she nursed from 1917 to 1919.

There is no doubt that her care was appreciated by soldiers convalescing both at Swinton Grange and in France. She received numerous letters and cards of thanks for her generous gifts of flowers, cigarettes, books, clothing and money which she sent to soldiers, as well as for her nursing care. She also joined her colleagues in entertainments and musical concerts for patients.

Even after her patients had been discharged from hospital, she maintained contact with them and their families, showing a thoughtful, compassionate interest in their long term welfare. In the case of one soldier who had died, she painstakingly arranged for his memorial stone to be moved to be near his family in Australia. His mother was very appreciative of Ursula's efforts on her behalf which involved numerous letters trying to cut through the red tape.

Private Gater (official portrait)

April 16th/15   Pte Y. Gater
9 Scotia Rd
Burslem
%
Nurse U. Lascelles
I am writing to tell you that
I received your letter and
am very pleased to hear from
you and I have got another
fortnights extension and I
am not going back yet I
have been to a Doctor and
he says it will take
months before it is ~~more~~ right
and I shall be very pleased

of anything of what you can
send they will be acceptible
and the socks about 7 inche
in the foot and please
remember me to your mother
I should have liked to have
seen you before I came away
but you must excuse me
for it couldnt be helped
and I am sorry about
the the men having to
go to Leeds again I am
enjoying myself very much
so I think I have said

all this time closing my
letter with best wishes
hoping to hear from you
soon

Pte Y. Gater

167

To
Miss Lacelles

Just a few lines to tell you
that i have got quite Setled
now i have had a good Look round
it is a very nice Place and the Sister &
nurces is very Kind to Every one & all is nice & comftable
i have meet some very nice Lads my bed is mate & Bradford
Lad he as Lost bath is feet with frost Bite and he
as got is ones on & he can walk very well with them
i hoped i shall do is good when i get mine, I have been
& Passed the Soctor to Day & he wanted to take some
more of mine but i told him i had 7 Operations & i dident
want anymore but if it was so i should want to go back
to St Barts Horpital so that i could have Capt Ball
to Do it and be Nursed with the Sister & Harley again but
when i told him that he sent for the Man of the firm
witch is making them & he said it just was to Let them alone
for he could fit me better with it on, You must Remberme
to your Mother and i will tell you all next time i
rite to you & Thanking you boath for all your
Kindness wils i was at Slingsby & Laiter Wished
to be rembered to you i think that is all this
time Yours Sencerly ————

R Fentiman

No 6436
S/Cpl R Fentiman
1 st East Yorkshire Regt
Ward 1
Roehampton House
Roehampton S.W)

R E Fentim—
1 st East Yor—

She was in constant correspondence with her nursing and medical colleagues. As a memento of her time in Rouen a colleague sent her an album with pictures depicting scenes of everyday life in the hospital, using a hectographic jelly process to print them.

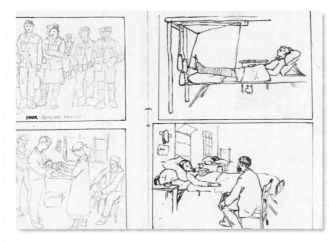

Ursula did have a period of illness herself, and was sent home from France to recuperate from "Rose Measles". This seems to have been what we now know as German Measles.

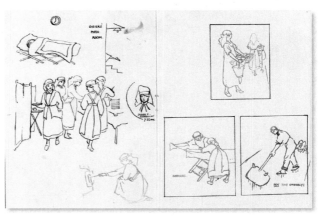

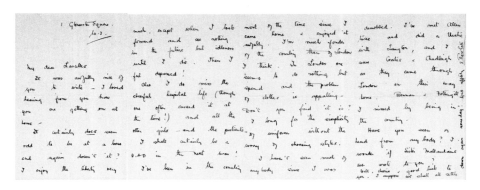

*See page 200 for transcript of part
of this letter.*

As her service ended, Ursula in common with many other nurses and VADs experienced feelings of great loneliness and uncertainty about her future life and work.

In 1921 a colleague wrote to her from Intarfa Hospital in Malta:-
"I am sure you miss hospital life but I don't think you would like it nearly as much in peace time as you get very little real nursing, whereas during the war you felt you were doing your best and were of some use to the poor Tommies, although it was all very sad, but I just loved it."

There was some ill feeling on Ursula's part about the treatment of the army service compared with volunteers and other ranks. She voiced her concerns in a letter to the local MP. Edmond Rossborough Turton in 1919, asking him to submit a question in the House of Commons about the members of the nursing service not receiving a months' leave on full pay on demobilisation as she understood was granted to other ranks.

The following poem sent to Ursula by one of her grateful patients sums up the affection in which all VAD nurses were held.

Wounded, sick, war worn and weary
Shivering from the wintery wind
Soldiers from the wastes so dreary
Come to hospital and find
Comfort and a welcome cheery from your sisters good and kind

From the ranks where men are broken
From the land of slush and mud
From the lines of fire and blood
Soldiers come from hell to heaven
Led by pure sweet sisterhood

Heaven bless you in your duty
Sisterhood of sterling worth
Ever tender, gentle, kindly
To sad hearts - new hopes give birth
Sister Lascelles and your comrades
Sure are angels in this earth.

Driver A.J Teale
Written on Australian Red Cross Paper

After the war Ursula continued to help her mother at home and, after their mother's death, lived with her brother in the house at Slingsby. Neither of them married. She still participated in Red Cross activities and was an enthusiastic fundraiser. She was an avid collector of letters and wrote articles in her scrapbooks about the village communities around her, with details about village events and personalities. It is obvious from looking through her archive material that she never threw anything away.

After her brother's death she lived alone in her house until she needed to live in a care home around the time of her 100th birthday. She died aged 102 but what a character she must have been and what a difference she must have made to so many lives!

In her writings she once wondered if anyone would ever read about her experiences We have been privileged to have some insight into her interesting life.

Thirsk Auxiliary Military Hospital

"Thirsk Auxiliary Military Hospital," Town Hall, Thirsk.

Date of opening	26th Nov. 1914.
Date of closing	8th February, 1919.
No. of Beds	65.
Total number of patients treated ...	1,014.
No. of deaths	One.
Hospital affiliated to ...	East Leeds War Hospital.
Commandant ...	A. C. Ferguson, Esq., M.D., O.B.E.
Hon. Commandant	Mrs. R. L. Bower.
Medical Officer	A. C. Ferguson, Esq., M.D., O.B.E., Thirsk.
Matron ...	Mrs. Pollard, A.R.R.C. (Honorary).
Quartermasters ...	Miss Edith Gilling and Miss Hilda Gilling.
Staffed by	Yorks./2 and Trained Nurses

Thirsk Town Hall was designed by Yorkshire architect by Walter Brierley opening in 1913 and within a year was pressed into service as a hospital.

The Commandant of the Men's Detachment was F. Darling Esq. of Sowerby Grange Thirsk. Dr. MacArthur acted as Medical Officer until he went on active service. He was followed by Dr. A.C. Ferguson whose son, Captain F.E. Ferguson died in October 1919 having been awarded the Military Cross. He is commemorated on the Thirsk war memorial.

In this early picture the lady in the darker uniform sitting on the steps was probably the Commandant Mrs. R.L. Bower. Her husband became the North Riding County Director in the latter years of the war. Note the use of flowers on the stage which is a typical feature of the VAD nurses trying to create a pleasant and homely atmosphere for the soldiers.

Yorks./2. Thirsk.

Commandant and Medical Officer : A. C. Ferguson, Esq., M.D., O.B.E.

Hon. Commandant : Mrs. R. L. Bower.

Name.	Record of War Service.	Part time or Whole time.
Gilling, Miss Edith ...	Quartermaster. Thirsk Hospital ..	Whole time
Gilling, Miss Hilda ...	Asst. do. ,, ...	Whole time
Bell, Miss Heather ..	Thirsk Hospital ..	Part time
Barley, Miss Frances ..	,, ...	,,
Dale, Miss Frances ..	,, ...	,,
Mott, Miss Irene ...	,, ...	,,
Stokes, Mrs. Mary ...	,, ...	,,
Thompson, Miss Evelyn ..	,, ...	,,
Wood, Miss Lucy ...	,, ...	,,
Walker, Mrs. Violet ...	,, ...	,,
Hutchinson, Miss Kate ...	,, ...	,,
Moss Miss Gertrude ...	,, ...	,,
Bower, Miss Constance	Thirsk Hospital ; also at Kings-wood Park Hospital, Tunbridge-Wells ...	,,
Talbot, Mrs. Geraldine ...	Thirsk Hospital ...	,,
Austen, Mrs. Phyllis ...	,, ...	,,
Cleasby, Miss Annie ...	,, ...	,,
Holyday, Mrs. Louisa ...	,, ...	,,
Danby, Miss Kathleen ...	,, ..	,,
Bateman, Mrs. Elizabeth ...	,, ...	,,
Windross, Mrs. Ellen ...	,, ...	,,
Watson, Mrs. Louisa ...	,, ...	,,
Ryder, Mrs. Alice ...	,, ...	,,
Brown, Mrs. Muriel ...	,, ...	,,
Richardson, Miss Evangeline ...	,, ...	,,
Scott, Miss Jessie ...	,, ...	,,
Robson, Miss Hilda ...	,, ...	,,
Horner, Mrs. Bel ...	,, ...	,,
Johnson, Miss Edith ...	,, ...	,,
Jackson, Miss Marie ...	,, ..	,,
Rymer, Miss Margaret ...	,, ...	,,
Jackson, Miss Esmé ...	,, ...	,,
Hansell, Miss Mary ...	,, ...	,,
Brooke, Miss Helen ...	,, ...	,,

Trained nurses were also employed.

The Thirsk men's detachment had a fluctuation of numbers over the years due to men enlisting and working in reserved occupations as the war progressed. Here is the report on their activities from the North Riding War Report book.

YORKS./1 V.A.D., THIRSK.

Commandant	-	F. DARLING, Esq.
Medical Officer		Dr. W. McARTHUR (on active service).

This Detachment during the year ending December, 1918, has done much useful service in providing escorts for conveying wounded soldiers, principally from East Leeds Military Hospital to most of the Auxiliary Hospitals in the Riding, and also to Wakefield, Hull, Harrogate, and Ilkley. The number of Orderlies supplied for this work, from January 3rd, 1918, to November 25th, is 107, and the number of Patients conveyed during the same period is 1,558.

In addition to these cases the Detachment has supplied Orderlies for the meeting and conveyance of Wounded Men from Thirsk Station to Thirsk Auxiliary Hospital, by means of Motor Ambulance and other conveyances, and also in removing men and stores from the Headquarters at Northallerton to Thirsk, Redcar, and Saltburn.

The Detachment has had regular meetings on Sunday afternoons and Tuesday evenings for Stretcher Drill, Practice, and Lectures in First Aid Work and Bandaging.

On the 23rd June an Inspection of the Detachment was held by Major-General Sir Walter Bedford, K.C.B., the D.D.M.S., and Major R. L. Bower, C.M.G., County Director, when 18 men were on parade. The work done on this occasion consisted of preparation of beds for hospital; and for a Camp the following preparations were made, viz.:—Water Supply, Incenerator, Latrine, Refuse Disposal, etc.

Various field dressings, stretcher carrying, loading ambulance, and transport to hospital were carried out.

On the 7th July a "Test Call Out" was made, when the Detachment assembled at the Racecourse, collected and applied the necessary dressings for ten cases, and then conveyed them to a train in waiting at Thirsk Railway Station, and loaded them into Railway Carriages. The work was satisfactorily done in about two hours under the inspection of the County Director.

The Detachment has been equipped with requirements necessary for the equipment of an Emergency Ambulance Train in the event of an Invasion, and on Sunday afternoon, 6th October, 1918, a practice was held when patients were removed from the Racecourse at Thirsk and loaded into Cattle Trucks and Railway Carriages from the ground level, the necessary equipment being taken in the Motor Ambulance.

It has always been on duty and ready for any emergency whenever warnings of Air Raids have been given.

It has supplied Orderlies for Red Cross Concerts, and organised and worked a Whist Drive by which the sum of £47 : 6 : 3 was raised for the "Our Day" Fund of the Red Cross Society.

It supplied for two weeks, night and day, two Orderlies at the Thirsk A.M.H. for restraint and in attendance on a serious case in which the patient was delirious.

For some weeks two Orderlies have attended the Thirsk Hospital on Sunday mornings to see dressings done and to gain experience. This is most useful to the members of the Detachment, and is much appreciated by them.

174

At the start of the war, soldiers sent home to convalesce from their injuries, wore their usual uniforms, which led to their being accused of "not doing their bit" for their country when they were seen out and about in their communities.

Jane Elizabeth Wilkinson, seen here preparing a rabbit. She had previously been a cook working for the Vicar at Topcliffe prior to the war.

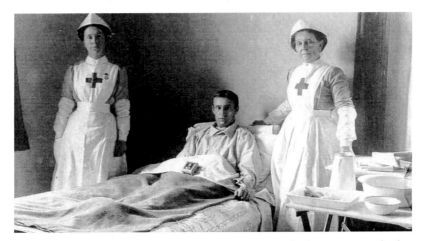

These VADs are wearing the 'Sister Dora' caps which were named after Dorothy Wyndlow Pattison, the daughter of the vicar Rev MJ Pattison of Hauxwell near Richmond. Born in 1832, Dorothy Pattison joined the sisterhood of the Good Samaritans at Coatham near Middlesbrough, where she became known as Sister Dora.
She was sent to Walsall where her dedicated nursing is commemorated by a statue, and numerous roads and hospitals named after her.

The uniform worn by these men was issued as the war progressed, preventing them from being accused of not fighting for their country when they were out in their communities.
Known as a 'bluey' it was a rough fitting suit of blue/grey cloth, with white lapels and worn with a red tie.
The VADs in this picture are wearing the head dress known as the veil, introduced in 1915.

Welburn Red Cross Hospital

"Welburn Hall Hospital." Kirbymoorside.

Building lent by ...	...	Mrs. Edward Shaw, O.B.E.
Date of opening ...	...	22nd May, 1917.
Date of closing ...	...	Still open.
No. of Beds ...	...	100.
Total number of patients treated to date ...		886
No. of deaths ...	...	One.
Hospital affiliated to ...		East Leeds War Hospital.
Commandant ...	...	Mrs. Edward Shaw, O.B.E.
Medical Officers ...	...	Dr. J. F. Porter, O.B.E.
		Dr. R. A. Jackson.
Hon. Secretary ...	...	Mr. Percy Smith.
Staffed by	...	Yorks./72, Trained Nurses and Masseuse.

This splendid Auxiliary Hospital is one of the very few remaining open in the Country. Extremely well equipped and staffed it has done invaluable work in treating both severe and convalescent cases. It is now being used by the Ministry of Pensions in response to an urgent request for Hospital accommodation.

Welburn Hall is a country house which was rebuilt by Walter Brierley between 1890-1893 on the site of an old hall which at one time belonged to Rievaulx Abbey. An extension was added in 1895 for Mr James Edward Shaw who then owned the house. It was partly rebuilt again after a fire in 1932 and in 1951 became a school for children with special needs, which still exists today.

James Shaw was married to Adela Constance Alexandrina Durrant, the daughter of the 4th Baronet Durrant of Scottow, Norfolk in 1892. They had a son John Edward Durrant Shaw but his father died in 1911. Adela Shaw offered the use of the hall at the outbreak of the war and became the Commandant.

At the end of the war Mrs Shaw was the founder of the Adela Shaw Hospital at Kirbymoorside and was a driving force behind the running of it, aided no doubt by her experiences running the Red Cross hospital at Welburn Hall. She was awarded the OBE for her work during the war and went on to become a Justice of the Peace, President of the Yorkshire Association of Women's Institute and finally CBE. She is credited with being responsible for reforming child health and welfare in the district at a time when 5000 children had been crippled with polio and TB.

The photos in this section came from this lovely album donated by a relative of one of the nurses.

Yorks./72. Kirkdale.

Commandant : Mrs, Edward Shaw, O.B.E.
Medical Officer : Dr. J. F. Porter, O.B.E.

Name.	Record of War Service.	Part time or Whole time.
Shaw, Mrs. Edward, O.B.E. ...	Duncombe Park and Welburn Hall Hospitals	Whole time
Powell, Mrs. Lilian	Quartermaster	Part time
Porter, Dr. J. Francis	,,	,,
Aydon, Mrs. Alice	,,	
Barker, Miss Edith	Welburn Hall Hospital	
Barker, Miss Ethel	Duncombe Park and Welburn Hall Hospital	
Barker, Mrs. Louie	Welburn Hall Hospital	
Bell, Miss Annie	Duncombe Park and Welburn Hall Hospital	
Bray, Mrs. Lily	,, ,, ,,	
Brown, Miss Evelyn	,, ,, ,,	
Bucktin, Miss Francis E.	Welburn Hall Hospital	
Cadman, Miss Eveline	Duncombe Park and Welburn Hall Hospital	
Carpenter, Miss Alice	,, ,, ,,	
Colley, Miss Hannah J.	,, ,, ,,	
Dixon, Miss Constance	,, ,, ,,	
Dodds, Miss Annie	,, ,, ,,	
Ford, Miss Christiana	Welburn Hall Hospital	
Hall, Miss Amy	Welburn Hall Hospital	
Hill, Miss Esther	Duncombe Park and Welburn Hall Hospital	
Hornby, Miss Mary	,, ,, ,,	
Huffington, Mrs. Kate	,, ,, ,,	
Marwood, Mrs. Harriet	,, ,, ,,	
Peacock, Miss Margery	,, ,, ,,	
Read, Miss Mary	,, ,, ,,	
Robinson, Miss Caroline	,, ,, ,,	
Sunley, Mrs. Jane	,, ,, ,,	
Stokell, Mrs. Jane	,, ,, ,,	
Swales, Miss Elsie	,, ,, ,,	
Slater, Mrs. Louisa	,, ,, ,,	
Warriner, Mrs. Eleanor	Welburn Hall Hospital	
Warriner, Miss Frances	Welburn Hall Hospital	
Wass, Miss Ellis	Duncombe Park and Welburn Hall Hospital	
Winnall, Mrs. Ada	Welburn Hall Hospital	
White, Mrs. Julia	Duncombe Park and Welburn Hall Hospital	
Wood, Miss Maggie	,, ,, ,,	

109.
Kirby Moorside   Welburn Hall -   Mrs E. Shaw.
                      Yorks.   Beds 100
Clarke Miriam   ??? 8.8.18 10.10.18

Typical ward scenes at Welburn Hall with yet more deer antlers above the beds.

Time for tea

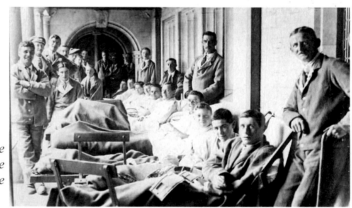

Some patients on the balcony taking in the beneficial Yorkshire air.

Wykeham Abbey Hospital

The first nine soldiers arrived here on 28th October 1914 and included 3 men from the Middlesex Regiment and 2 from the Royal Irish. From this date soldiers arrived on almost a weekly basis for the next 4 years. They are all recorded in the Wykeham Abbey Visitors book and come from all over Britain, Ireland, Canada and South Africa. It is possible that some civilians were also treated as there is a photograph of a Reverend H Simpson who was saved from the Lusitania when the ship was torpedoed in 1915.

The Malton Messenger of 21st November 1914 reported "13 wounded soldiers arrived at Wykeham Abbey by the 4 o'clock train from Scarborough. The men were met at the station by Dr Hardwicke and members of the St John Ambulance. A motor ambulance was also brought for those who were unable to walk. Several of the soldiers were

Yorks/12. West Ayton.

Commandant: The Hon. Norah Dawnay.
Medical Officer: Dr. W. Sibbald-Robertson.

Name.	Record of War Service.	Part time or Whole time.
Dawnay, The Hon. Norah ...	Commandant. Wykeham Abbey Hospital	Full time
Sibbald-Robertson, Dr. William	Medical Officer. ,, ,, ...	Part time
Tilly, Mrs. Mary ...	Trained Nurse ,, ,, ...	,,
Cooper, Miss Norah ...	Red Cross Hospital, Etherley, Durham	Whole time
Douglass, Miss Noel ...	Red Cross Hospital, Exmouth	,,
Stapleton, Miss Jean ...	Red Cross Hospital, Etherley, Durham	,,
Armitage, Miss Daisy ..	Wykeham Abbey Hospital	,,
Armitage, Miss Kitty ..	,, ,, ...	Part time
Barber, Miss Mary ...	,, ,, ...	,,
Collins, Miss Elsie ...	Tooting War Hospital and York Military War Hospital ...	Whole time
Darry, Miss Edith Margaret ...	Bilton Hall Red Cross Hospital	Part time
Dear, Miss Mary ...	Wykeham Abbey Hospital	,,
Collinson (nee M. Glaves), Mrs.	5th Northern General Hospital, Leicester	Whole time
Fitch, Miss Marjorie ...	Wykeham Abbey Hospital	Part time
Flint, Miss Beatrice ...	Cambridge War Hospital	Whole time
Eaton (nee Edith Jackson), Mrs.	Wykeham Abbey Hospital	Part time
Jackson, Miss Mary ...	,, ,, ...	,,
Jackson, Miss Kitty ...	,, ,, ...	,,
Jewitt, Miss Annie ...	,, ,, ...	,,
Monkman, Miss Lauretta ...	,, ,, ...	,,
Jennings (nee Sarah Noble), Mrs	2nd Western General Hospital, Manchester	Whole time
Raine, Miss Annie ...	Wykeham Abbey Hospital	Part time
Stead, Mrs. Constance ..	,, ,, ...	,,
Stevenson, Miss Adelaide ..	,, ,, ...	,,
Taylor, Miss Charlotte ..	,, ,, ...	,,
Taylor, Miss Janet Everley ...	La Tonquet, France, etc.	Whole time
Ward, Mrs. Vera ...	Huddersfield War Hospital ; Ripon Military Hospital ...	,,
White, Miss Ellen ...	Rugely Camp, Hospital	,,
White, Miss Doris ...	Wykeham Abbey Hospital	Part time
Wilkinson, Miss Lydia ...	5th Northern General Hospital, Leicester	Whole time

removed on stretchers to the motor. There are now 22 soldiers at the Abbey, which Viscount Downe has placed at the disposal of the Government."

In the North Riding financial reports for 1915 there is mention that drugs for Wykeham Abbey Hospital cost £6-12s-4d. At times there were almost 70 wounded soldiers being treated at the hospital. The Brown Drawing Room was renamed Number 1 Ward for the duration of the war.

Pte Carney   Pte Henderson

Hon. Faith Dawnay, a member of the family who had been a nurse and ambulance driver in the French army, for which she received the Croix de Guerre, returned to Wykeham Abbey possibly needing rest after being wounded. She became involved as a nurse there when she had recovered. She was awarded a War Medal along with the Hon. Norah Dawnay for their hospital work.

Other members of the nursing team receiving honours for their work in the war according to War Office reports were Miss B Newman and Miss D Armitage.

Lord Downe's Great Aunt Ruth, aged 8 years, taking Bandsman W.E. Harvey of the Gloucester Regiment out for a drive.

Another outing by some interesting transportation.

Sister Crouch, whose autograph is in this visitor's book staff page, proved to be a heroine on Christmas morning 1917 when she extinguished a fire in the billiard room at 1.30 am. That evening she was presented with a medal in appreciation of her calmness and prompt action. On New Year's Day Sergeant Tippen presented her with an attache case on behalf of the patients.

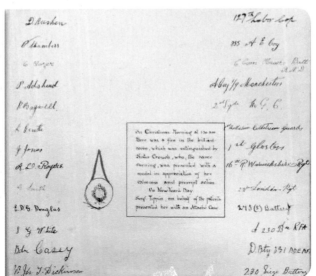

One of the Men's Yorks/27 West Ayton VAD Detachment members, Thomas Willings passed his first aid examination in 1913.

Music played a large part in the entertainment of soldiers. A concert was given by some patients and members of staff to raise funds for the re-covering of the billiard table. There were songs, carols, a violin solo and a monologue ending with "God Save The King." The charge was 1 penny and £9-16s-2d was raised.

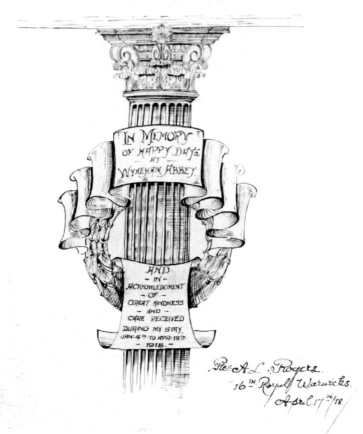

In Memory
of Happy Days
at
Wylehan Abbey

And
- in -
Acknowledgment
- of -
Great Kindness
- and -
Care Received
During My Stay,
Jan: 4th to Apr: 18th
1918.

Pte. A. L. Rogers.
16th Royal Warwicks.
April 17th/18

There are large numbers of cartoons and dedications in the visitors'
book and here are two examples of wonderful artwork by soldiers.

Pte. H Wheen W Yorks & Lanks
April 23rd 1917

Wydale Hall Hospital

Wydale Hall is a listed 18th century building in the foothills of the North York Moors National Park in the Vale of Pickering. Originally it was owned by George Cayley, the aviation pioneer and then in the 1900s it was sold to the Illingworth family who loaned it to the Red Cross as a hospital in the first world war. The house is set in 14 acres of gardens and woodland. and is now a retreat and diocesan centre.

It was reported that soldiers were moved to Wydale from a Scarborough hospital to make room for wounded civilians from the German bombardment of the town in 1914.

Mrs Illingworth, the Commandant, wrote to the Red Cross offering the house as a hospital and kept an album of letters, soldiers' and nurses' details including medical records and newspaper cuttings of the time some of which are reproduced overleaf. The album is in the British Red Cross Archives Department.

Those with Red X Flag.

Our ambulance for 4 stretchers

Sands. Lewis - Mitcham - Mahoney - Gillett.

A Wydale Snowdrift 1915.

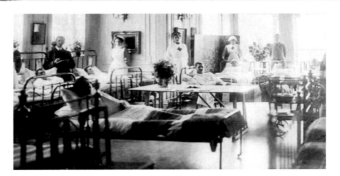

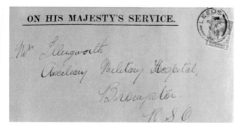

What excitement there must have been on the receipt of this telegram! This was the usual method of communication between the military hospitals and the auxiliary hospitals.

Telephone No.
Regent 6151 (7 lines)
Telegraphic Address:
"Assistance, Charles London."

Any further communication on this subject should be addressed to
THE SECRETARY,
and the following number quoted

Ref. No. M.45.

BRITISH RED CROSS SOCIETY,

Incorporated by Royal Charter, 1908.

83, PALL MALL,

LONDON, S.W.

3rd November 1914

Dear Madam:

I beg to inform you that your generous offer of Hospital accommodation has been approved by the Military Authorities, and this decision has been communicated to the General Officer Commanding-in-Chief   Northern   Command - All future communications should be made to this Officer through your County Director.

Due notice will be given to you when it is necessary for you to prepare beds for the reception of patients.

Yours faithfully,

Frank Hastings

The nursing staff were privately obtained by Mrs Illingworth and included herself and her two daughters. There were also three trained nurses, Sister Edda Reid, Sister Matilda Letitia King, and Sister Rose Willis. The autographs of George Hardwick and Frank Godfrey who were the doctors involved in the hospital are also here.

A soldier's story at Wydale.

The newspaper cutting describing the wounding of Private Archibald Cairns at Ypres on November 1st 1914.

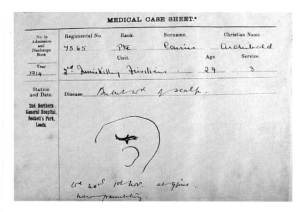

MEDICAL CASE SHEET.*

No. in Admission and Discharge Book	Regimental No.	Rank.	Surname.	Christian Name.
7565	Pte	Cairns	Archibald

Private Cairns was admitted to Wydale Hospital from 2nd Northern General Hospital, Becketts Park, Leeds. He was 29 years old and had served for 3 years in the army.

He was suffering from a bullet wound to his scalp which can be seen on his medical card filled in on his admission.

Private Cairns is on the left side of the front row with the bandage round his head and dog on his lap.

Here he is, much improved, in the centre front with bulldog.

193

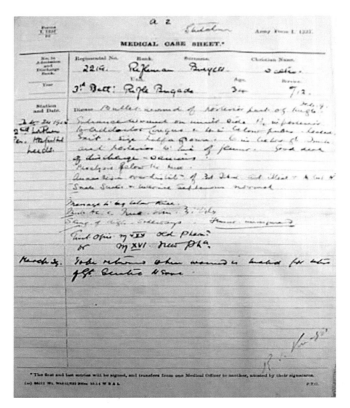

Another medical care sheet. It is interesting to note that doctor's writing was incredibly hard to read in those days too!

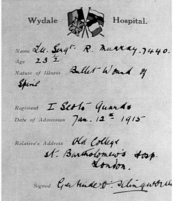

Name *Lt. Sergt. R. Murray. 7440.*
Age *23½*
Nature of Illness *Bullet Wound of Spine*

Regiment *I Scots Guards*
Date of Admission *Jan. 12th 1915*

Relative's Address *Old College St. Bartholomew's Hosp. London.*

Signed *Gertrude Illingworth*

BRITISH RED CROSS SOCIETY,

Incorporated by Royal Charter, 1908.

83, PALL MALL,

LONDON, S.W.

1st May 1915

Telephone:
REGENT 6131 (6 lines)
Telegraphic Address:
"Assistance Charles, London."

Any further communication on this subject should be addressed to
THE SECRETARY
and the following number quoted—

Room 91

Dear Madam,

I beg to acknowledge the receipt of your letter, informing me that your Hospital is to be closed on June ~~11th~~ 1st. This fact shall be duly noted in our books and the War Office shall be informed.

May I take the opportunity of offering you the cordial thanks of the Society for the generous and patriotic assistance which you have rendered to the sick and wounded soldiers.

Yours faithfully

p.p. F. Hastings

Secretary
R.F.T.

The letter acknowledging the closure of the hospital in 1915.

195

Some Souvenirs

Embroidered post cards sent by soldiers

These postcards were hand or machine embroidered by women and war orphans in Paris, and were also produced in Belgium, and in Switzerland.

They were sold everywhere from tiny village shops to big city stores, and cost between 1 and 3 francs each, depending on the intricacy of the embroidery. (The average British Tommy received about 10 shillings, almost 10 francs, each week.)

The most popular cards had sentimental messages with pretty flowers and scenes depicted. Those with Regimental badges were particularly prized, as were those with an envelope like flap which contained a small greeting card.

Treasured by the recipients, the cards were often framed to be kept by the families at home.

Princess Mary Brass Box

In November 1914, an advertisement was placed in the national press inviting monetary contributions to a 'Sailors & Soldiers Christmas Fund' which had been created by Princess Mary, the seventeen year old daughter of King George V and Queen Mary. The purpose was to provide everyone wearing the King's uniform and serving overseas on Christmas Day 1914 with a 'gift from the nation'.

The response was truly overwhelming, and it was decided to spend the money on an embossed brass box, based on a design by Messrs Adshead and Ramsey. The contents varied considerably; officers and men on active service afloat or at the front received a box containing a combination of pipe, lighter, 1 oz of tobacco and twenty cigarettes in distinctive yellow monogrammed wrappers. Non-smokers and boys received a bullet pencil and a packet of sweets instead. Indian troops often got sweets and spices, and nurses were treated to chocolate. Many of these items were despatched separately from the tins themselves, as once the standard issue of tobacco and cigarettes was placed in the tin there was little room for much else apart from the greeting card.

H.R.H. THE PRINCESS ROYAL

At The End of the War

At the conclusion of the war, the North Riding Red Cross made arrangements for the disposal of equipment from the hospitals, reallocation of funds which remained, and the continuation of the service in the North Riding.

VAD Statistics WW1

Just before the declaration of War, these were the numbers of Detachments and personnel in the country as a whole:

	DETACHMENTS		PERSONNEL	
	B.R.C.S	St John	B.R.C.S	St John
Women	1,582	241	40,018	6,773
Men	408	143	17,666	5,865
Total	1,990	384	57,714	12,683

At the date of the Armistice, these figures had increased as below:-

	DETACHMENTS		PERSONNEL	
	B.R.C.S	St John	B.R.C.S	St John
Women	2,534	713	66,211	24,440
Men	560	276	24,712	10,630
Total	3,094	989	90,923	35,070

Total Nursing Members posted up to 20 December 1919	17,367
Total General Service Members	11,000
Joint War Committee Hospitals' Members	1,755
HONOURS	
Nursing Members Mentioned in Despatches	886
Nursing Decorations	329
General Service Members, Mentioned in Despatches	103
General Service Members, Decorations	1
Joint War Committee Hospitals' Members, Mentioned in Despatches	103
Joint War Committee Hospitals' Members, Decorations	34
DEATHS	
Nursing Members*	128
General Service Members	11
Joint War Committee Hospitals' Members	6

*It is known that over 100 other VAD members, not working directly under the V.A. Department, also laid down their lives

Scholarships awarded to VADs for further professional training after the war: 557."

Source: Joint War Committee and the Joint War Finance Committee of the British Red Cross Society and the Order of St John of Jerusalem in England on Voluntary Aid rendered to the Sick and Wounded at Home and Abroad and to British Prisoners of War, 1914-1919' Part V111 Published HMSO, 1921)

The County Director in the North Riding Major R.L. Bowers in 1920 reported:

V.A. Detachments.
"There are now 19 Men's Detachments in the Riding, with a total of 689 Officers and men. One or two Detachments are rather low in numbers, but the majority are well up to strength, very keen and efficient.

During the war a very large number of our men enlisted, and about 20 others volunteered and were accepted for service in Hospitals at home and abroad. The Detachments performed a splendid amount of work, acting as orderlies in Auxiliary Hospitals, escorting patients to and from the Base Hospitals, driving Motor Ambulances, and duty during Air-Raids, etc. The loyalty and harmonious co-operation which has existed throughout the war between the Officers and Members of Detachments is most gratifying, and has tended very largely to the efficient and valuable work which has been done, very often at great personal sacrifice.

The Women's Detachments now number 40 with a total of 1,492 Officers and Members. No praise can be too high for the majority of VAD workers for the long and excellent service they rendered, not only by staffing our Red Cross Hospitals in the Riding but no fewer than 499 volunteered and were accepted for service in Military Hospitals, hospital ships and trains, both at home and abroad. I am proud to say that the members who served away proved themselves highly satisfactory and a credit to their County.

Hospitals
Our Hospitals were extremely well maintained with all possible economy and care, and the work carried out to the entire satisfaction of Headquarters, Northern Command, to whom we were partly responsible. The credit for this state of things is very largely due to the Commandants, every one of whom gave their service gratuitously and whole-heartedly, and to the Quartermasters who were responsible to the Commandant for keeping of lists of furniture, stores, linen, accounts, etc. We also owe a very large debt of gratitude to the Medical Officers and Trained Nurses, on whom so much depended for the successful treatment of patients."

The 32 hospitals in the County had 1,454 equipped beds, and the total number of patients treated was 18,422

Mural Tablets.
It was suggested that a mural tablet should be presented to the owners of each building which had been occupied as a hospital.
The wording was to be:

"Lest we forget"
1914 - 1919

"This building which was equipped and staffed by the British Red Cross manned by North Yorkshire .... Voluntary Aid Detachments was used as an Auxiliary Hospital for sick and wounded sailors and soldiers during the Great War 1914 to 1919 during which period ....patients were treated."

Finally a national initiative created a beautifully illustrated scroll which was sent to each hospital in the Country accompanied by a letter of thanks signed by Winston Churchill (Secretary of State for War)

The scroll displayed at Wykeham Abbey

VAD Nurses.
"Many women returning home after the conflict ended undertook formal nurse train-ing and registration with the G.N.C. Others tried to pick up the threads of their former lives. What must be certain is that life could never be the same for any of them again. The sight, smell, and fear of war must have been imprinted on every mind, bringing about a change in the lives of women which would grow and grow over the following years"

In the collection of Ursula Lascelle's correspondence, letters from her friends de-scribe the loneliness and sadness after finishing work as a VAD. One such letter from S Rowlatt (nurse) reads:-
" It certainly does seem odd to be at a loose end again doesn't it? I enjoy the Liberty very much except when I look forward and see nothing in the future but idleness until I die. Then I feel depressed!
Also I do miss the cheerful hospital life (though one cursed it at the time) and all the other girls and the patients. I shall certainly be a VAD in the next war! ....
The problem of clothes is appalling. Don't you find it is? I long for the simplicity of uniform without the worry of choosing styles.
...........I suppose we shall all settle down again some day"

This feeling of uncertainty was not unique to the VADs. In 1918 Cicely Hamilton (recognised authority on women's topics) suggested "that the effect of the war and the next generation will be bad because with the flower of young manhood gone and the strength of the young womanhood overtaxed, the children born over the next few years may be of a nervous type." She anticipated "a temporary revival of femininity as distinguished from feminism."

Recognition of the service which the VADs had given was shown in the honours bestowed upon them. All VADs who had served in the UK for at least 1000 hours and ambulance drivers and bearers who had given 500 hours unpaid service received a War Medal. On one side was the Geneva cross with the words "For War Service 1914-18" and on the reverse "In-ter Arma Caritas", the Red Cross motto meaning "In War, Chari-ty".

Lady Florence Bell, as President of the North Riding Branch of the British Red Cross throughout the war, and Commandant of Roun-ton Red Cross Auxiliary Hospital was awarded the D.B.E. Other Commandants and medical officers received the O.B.E. Funds were raised to help nurses in financial need with the North Riding Branch donating £1,138-17s-1d to the "Nations Fund for the Nurses"

Grants
At the end of the war Sir Henry Beresford-Peirse was appointed by the North Riding Branch of the British Red Cross as one of the Trustees who administered the grant of £11,500 which had been sanctioned by the Joint War Commission. This money was to be used "to improve the arrangements for dealing with the relief of sickness and suffering".
The North Ormesby Hospital received £8,000, the North Riding Nursing Services Association £2,700, Rutson Hospital, Northallerton £300, Scarborough Nursing Association £300, and the Cottage Hospital, Malton £200.

Field Days
Training for VADs continued, including Field Days, as recorded in the final report below:

"On Saturday, July 26th, 1919, a Field Day took place at Northallerton. There were 60 Detachments on parade, numbering 973 Men, Women, and Officers.

During the morning, competitions for the "Lady Bell Cup" and "Sir Willans Nussey Cup" were conducted by R.A.M.C. Officers under the direction of Major General J. Thompson, C.B., C.M.G., the D.D.M.S. Northern Command, York. The following was the result:-

Winners of the Lady Bell Cup
Women
1. Yorks./12, West Ayton.
The Hon. Norah Dawnay, Commandant.
2. Yorks./52, Malton.
Miss A. Lupton, Commandant
3. Yorks./22, Scarborough.
Miss A. Tindall, Commandant

Winners of the Sir Willans Nussey Cup
Men
1. Yorks./33, Middlesbrough.
F.P.Wilson, Esq., Commandant
2. Yorks./29 Middlesbrough.
Dr. Hy. Ellis, Commandant
3. Yorks./15, Cloughton.
Dr. B.G. Forman, Commandant

After the Detachments had been inspected by Lieut. General Sir F. Ivor Maxse, K.C.B., C.V.O., D.S.O., General Officer Commanding-in-Chief, Northern Command, York, Sir Hugh Bell, Part, C.B., H.M. Lieut., and Lady Bell, D.B.E., the cups were presented by the Hon. Sir Arthur Stanley, G.B.E., C.B., M.V.O., M.P., Chairman of the Joint Committee of the British Red Cross Society and the Order of St. John of Jerusalem, who addressed the Detachments and thanked them on behalf of the Joint Committee for their very excellent services during the War."

Demobilisation
The County Director for the North Riding again reported:

With the single exception of Welburn Hall the whole of our Red Cross Hospitals in the Riding are now closed. In the case of the Hospital mentioned, Mrs. Edward Shaw, the Commandant, has very kindly offered it to the Ministry of Pensions and it has been accepted by them for the treatment of Pensioners. This beautiful Hospital is the most excellently equipped and staffed in every possible way, and is likely to be utilized by the Ministry of Pensions for some time to come.

As Hospitals closed, a very large accumulation of equipment of all kinds had to be disposed of in various ways, dilapidations made good, and matters settled generally between us and the people who have lent buildings, etc.

The Joint Committee in London promoted a Bill in the House of Commons, now the British Red Cross Society and Order of St. John Act, 1918.

If this Bill had not been passed it would not have been able to dispose of any of our property except for the specific purpose for which it was given to us, viz.:- for the treatment of sick and wounded soldiers; but under the Act we were able to give away, subject to the approval of the Demobilisation Committee, any of the property to Bodies or Institutions for the relief of sick or suffering in any form; preference being given to discharged Sailors and Soldiers.

The winding-up of the Hospitals entailed a considerable amount of work. Each Commandant was required to furnish me with an accurate and detailed inventory of all stores, equipment, etc., and the Commandants were also asked for their recommendations as regards the disposal of equipment to local Hospitals. As an initial step, Commandants were asked to return all articles which had been lent, and to hand over all perishable stores to their local or nearest Hospitals.

No equipment has been sold, except absolute Jumble, or goods which were not required in civilian Hospitals.

Disposal of Hospital Equipment.

The equipment was equally divided, according to the number of established beds, between the following Hospitals and Homes-

Scarborough.	The Sea Bathing Infirmary.
	Children's Homes.
	Cottage Hospital.
	Nursing Association.
Malton.	Cottage Hospital
	Nursing Association.
Northallerton.	Rutson Hospital.
	N.R. Nursing Association.
	Fever Hospital.
	Workhouse.
Thirsk.	Lambert Hospital.
	District Nursing Association.
Middlesbrough.	North Riding Infirmary.
	North Ormesby Infirmary.
	Workhouse Infirmary.
	Nursing Association.
	Sailors' Homes.
	Girls' Homes.
Brotton.	Miners' Hospital.
Marske-by-the-sea.	Miners' Hospital.
Guisbrough.	Cottage Hospital.
	Miners' Hospital.
London.	Royal Waterloo Hospital.
	Hospital for the Dying.
York.	The County Hospital.
	The Fever Hospital.
	The Military Hospital.
	Fairfield Sanatorium.
Scorton.	Hospital of St. John.
Easingwold.	Cottage Hospital.
Hinderwell.	Grinkle Miners' Hospital.
Morris Grange Sanatorium.	
Helmsley and Kirbymoorside.	The Nursing Association.
	Sisters of the Poor.
	Ryedale Cottage Hospital.
Saltburn and Skelton.	Pensioners' Hostel.
	Nursing Association.
	Miners' Hospital.
Masham.	The Isolation Hospital.
	Poor of the District.

Whitby.	Cottage Hospital.
	Nursing Association.
	Workhouse.
	Seamen's Institute.
	Lythe Nursing Association.
Richmond.	Fever Hospital.
	Victoria Hospital.
	Workhouse.

Stockton and Thornaby Hospital.
The R.A.F. Hospital, Marske.

We were able almost entirely to equip Morris Grange Hospital for Tuberculosis. This Hospital is to be used for Discharged Soldiers and Children, and is now under the control of the North Riding County Council. We also gave a large amount of furniture, bedsteads, bedding, medical stores, etc. to Fairfield Hospital, near York, a Hospital of 80 beds for Discharged Turbercular Soldiers. We have lent a large amount of hospital equipment, furniture, etc. to the R.A.F. Hospital, Marske, and the Military Hospital and G.S.V.A.D. Hospital, Catterick Camp."

Aid in Grants.
The balance sheet of the North Riding accounts had to give financial details of the closure of the hospital, with any credit balance being paid into the North Riding Hospital Fund, as approved by the Charity Commissioners.

As well as equipment being given away, grants amounting to £2,365 were distributed to many hospitals in the North Riding, including the Rutson Hospital in Northallerton. In this hospital wounded and discharged soldiers were cared for not under the direct control of the British Red Cross, but with their financial support. At the end of the war, the Rutson provided workshops on the hospital premises for wounded men. A grant of a further £300 was given in recognition of the care given to the wounded servicemen as sanctioned by the Joint War Committee in London.

V.A.Detachments who needed funds were also given financial support and a grant of £25 each was given to Northallerton, Richmond, Carlin How, Pickering and Redcar for the upkeep of Motor Ambulances.

Motor Ambulances.
"At the request of the Central Joint Committee in London, we have placed Motor Ambulances in various parts of the Riding for civilian use, and also for the transport of pensioners, Sailors and Soldiers, when necessary.

A small charge of 1/3 per mile is made, which covers the cost of Driver, Petrol, Oil, Attendant, etc., the County Director having power to remit the charge in cases of emergency or when the circumstances of the patient make it desirable.

All the Ambulances are fitted with the Standard War Office type body, and are capable of taking 4 stretcher cases or 8 sitters. Altogether we have 12 Ambulances, including two belonging to Mrs. Edward Shaw who has kindly placed them at our disposal.

The Ambulances are stationed at –

South Bank Gasworks
Welburn Hall, Kirbymoorside
Malton
Pickering
Whitby
Richmond
Bolckow Vaughan's Works, Dock Street, Middlesbrough
Redcar
Northallerton
Middlesbrough Fire Station.

So that practically the whole of the Riding is provided for.

Dilapidations
The question of dilapidations was given very careful consideration by Mr. Brierley, our County Surveyor. In some cases the owners of the buildings very generously made no claim for dilapidations.

I would specially like to mention Lord and Lady Normanby, Major and the Hon. Mrs. Clive Behrens, Mr. and Mrs. A.E. Kitching, and Mr. And Mrs. Lionel Dugdale, who not only organised and maintained their own Hospitals without any grant or subscription whatever, but made no claim for dilapidations.

On the question of dilapidations I am happy to say Mr. Brierley was able to report that very little damage had been done to the buildings, and the amount of repairs assessed by him was, in the majority of cases, very light.
People have been most generous to us throughout the War and it was only right and just that they should not be put to any expense in renovation".

Reconstruction.
It was hoped that the successful collaboration between the British Red Cross and the Order of St. John of Jerusalem would continue and develop to include such services as:-
    Child Welfare
    Work Parties to provide necessary garments for hospitals and health institutions
    Home Service Ambulance work
    Red Cross War and Peace Library
    Such care as may be necessary for prisoners of War

In Conclusion Major Bower wrote,

"I should like to express my most sincere gratitude to all those who have worked with me during the War.

To the Vice-Presidents, Commandants, Medical Officers, Men and Women of the Detachments, I am very grateful for their kind help and the kind consideration they have always shown me.

I should like to add how much we are indebted to Mr. W.S. Charlton, who audited our Accounts every year gratuitously. Also to Capt. And Mrs. G.J.E. Gardner who undertook the distribution of sugar to all our Hospitals from 1916 until the end of the War. This work was no light task and involved a good deal of time and labour – which was always so readily given.

R.L. Bower, Major
County Director.

North Riding Branch Headquarters,
The British Red Cross Office,
Police Buildings,
Northallerton. June, 1920.

In June 1925 the honour of Knight Commander of the Order of the British Empire was conferred by the King on Major R.L. Bower. Sir Robert had a distinguished career in military and civil life and was created C.M.G. in 1897 and CBE in 1920.

He served as Chief Constable in the North Riding from 1896 and was administrative commandant with the British Expeditionary Force in France 1914-1916.

In Northallerton he was presented with a cheque and an illuminated address by Lady Bell DBE JP, President of the North Riding Branch of British Red Cross Society, which expressed the esteem and regard in which they held him.

The final report of Lady Florence Bell, President of the North Riding branch of the British Red Cross.

1
INTRODUCTORY.

It is fitting, at the close of these years of strenuous service that those who have helped to steer the Red Cross movement in the North Riding should join in expressing their deep sense of indebtedness for the services which the North Riding Branch has so efficiently rendered.

As President of the Branch, whose privilege it has been to be connected with the movement since its first inception in 1907, I desire to associate myself with the County Director in his expression of admiration and gratitude for the work achieved under his guidance by the Voluntary Aid Detachments of the North Riding during the War.

The memories of the pre-war times during which the Red Cross activities were being gradually established and consolidated throughout the Riding, have been overlaid, and blurred perhaps, by the sterner realities of the years of War. But the hundreds of willing workers whose doings are recorded in the following pages, look back to those earlier days as the times of preparation which helped to make possible the great work subsequently accomplished. The fact that this work was done in almost every case on a voluntary basis, but nevertheless carried out with businesslike regularity and application, testifies to the steadfast and patriotic devotion of the workers. The fact that a loosely-knit voluntary organisation, complying willingly with regulations that there was no real power of enforcing, remained closely united until the end, and achieved signal success, testifies not only to the good will of the Branch but to the skill and tact of the County Director.

He succeeded during the last three years of the struggle, when the strength and nerves of even the sturdiest of the workers was showing signs of strain, in keeping the Branch at a high level of efficiency, and in steering it to the satisfaction of the whole Riding. His services, given voluntarily, were untiring in the administration of the Hospitals during the War. The amount of arranging and clearing-up afterwards, when the Hospitals were being demobilised, entailed on him as much work, and of a very exacting kind, as the supervision of the Hospitals when in being. In this task of demobilisation he was ably helped by the County Secretary, Miss Stainthorp, to whom all our thanks are due for the competent and unwearying work which her thorough grasp of all matters connected with the Branch enabled her to accomplish.

Although that phase of the Red Cross work is closed which dealt with the sick and wounded men from our fighting Armies—we pray that the need for it may never recur—let us not think that our labours are over. We stand on the threshold of future activities, almost as much needed as those which it has been our privilege to exercise in the past. Now is the time for the Commandants to do their utmost to keep their Detachments together, and to inspire them by advice and example to go forward in the same spirit as before.

On page 13 of the Report will be found a list of some of the further opportunities of public service offered to the members of our Detachments, by a great number of whom they will be eagerly welcomed.

2

The lives of many many women, of every station, who worked in our hospitals during the War, have been permanently leavened by that time of close intercourse and companionship with their fellow-workers. The added comprehension of one another, and the enduring sympathy evoked by it, will always remain a precious asset in their lives, whether that intercourse was in one of our country towns where workers of every kind and calling came out of their homes or places of business to take up the Hospital work, or in one of the villages scattered over the North Riding, in which the ties uniting the little community were drawn still closer by the work daily shared.

The sense of solidarity and fellowship which has permeated the North Riding Branch of the Red Cross during the War must not be allowed to lapse. Let it now serve as a basis for those further schemes of usefulness so much needed by the community in these days of upheaval.

It will be a pride and satisfaction to all the members of the Branch if we succeed in co-operating in these new phases of work upon which we are asked to enter, and in maintaining unbroken our tradition of faithful service.

FLORENCE BELL,

President of the North Riding Branch,

B.R.C.S.

June, 1920.

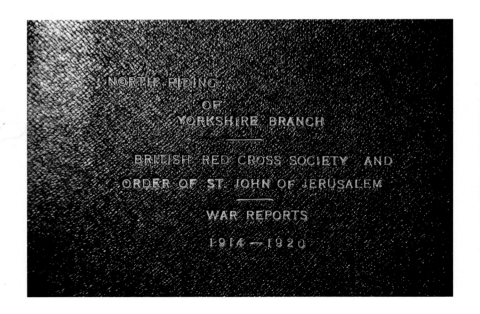

THIS BUILDING
WAS USED
DURING THE GREAT WAR AS
AN AUXILIARY RED CROSS
HOSPITAL FROM 25 NOV 1914
WHEN IT WAS OPENED TILL
3 JAN 1919 WHEN IT WAS FINALLY
CLOSED 387 SICK & WOUNDED
SOLDIERS WERE TENDED HERE
BY THE WOMEN OF THE VOLUNTARY
AID DETACHMENT YORKS 44 DRAWN
FROM THE VILLAGES OF EAST AND
WEST ROUNTON HARLSEY
INGLEBY CROSS & WELBURY

*In July 1920 this bronze memorial tablet was unveiled in the
Village Hall, East Rounton by Lady Bell.
The Rev. G. Bird read a prayer and a hymn followed. Sir Hugh Bell,
Major Bower, County Director, and Mr. Joseph Constantine joined
the many inhabitants of the Rountons who attended.*

209

Bibliography

John Pemberton. Will Pickles of Wensleydale. Geoffrey Bles 1970

Herman Senn. British Red Cross Society Cookery Manual no. 5. Cassell and company Ltd. 1913

James Cantlie. British Red Cross Society Nursing Manual no. 2 Cassell and Company Ltd. 1913

James Cantlie. British Red Cross Training Manual no.3 Cassell and Company Ltd. 1912

Florence Nightingale. Notes on Nursing. Harrison and sons. 1909

Joyce Denys, Gordon Hampden and Tindall M.C. Our Hospital ABC 3rd edition . The Bodley Head 1917

Amanda Bradley and Howard Watson. Stanley Spencer Heaven in a Hell of War. Pallant House Gallery 2013

Alison S. Fell and Christine E. Hallett. First World War Nursing. New Perspectives . Routledge Oxford 2013

Christine Hallett. Containing Trauma . Nursing Work in the First World War. Manchester University Press 2009

Ruth Cowen in association with Imperial War Museum. A Nurse at the Front – The First World War Diaries of Sister Edith Appleton. Simon and Schuster UK Ltd. 2013

Lynn Macdonald . The Roses of no Man's Land. Penguin Books London 2013

Melissa Larner, James Peto and Nadine Monem, War and Medicine Black Dog Publishing. London 2008

British Red Cross Society and Order of St. John of Jerusalem . War Reports 1914 – 1920. Original unpublished copy.

Ed. By J.A. Hammerton The War Illustrated . A pictorial Record of the Conflict of the Nations vols 1-9. The Amalgamated Press Ltd.

The History of the War Vol. 6. The Times 1916

Emily Wood The Red Cross Story A Pictorial History of 125 years of The British Red Cross. Dorling Kindersley 1995

Women at War. Voices from the Twentieth Century . Eye witness accounts from Imperial War Museum sound archive. Michael O' Mara Books Ltd. 2002

Michael Orr and James Crathorne. A Present from Crathorne. A Pictorial History of the North Yorkshire village of Crathorne. Crathorne Hall Hotel Yarm. 2000

E. Charles Vivian and J.E. Hodder Williams. The Way of the Red Cross. Hodder and Stoughton 1915

Susan Cohen. Medical Services in the First World War. Shire Library 2014

Neil R. Storey and Molly Housego. Women in the First World War. Shire Library 2010

Dame Beryl Oliver GBE RRC The British Red Cross in Action. Faber and Faber 1966

Stella Bingham . Ministering Angels. Osprey Publishing Ltd. 1979

Emily Mayhew. Wounded. The Long Journey Home From the Great War. Vintage Books 2014

Thelka Bowser. The Story of the British V.A.D. work in the Great War . Dept. of printed books, Imperial War Museum 2003.

William Robertson (compiler) "Middlesbrough's Efforts in the Great War" Jordison and Co.Ltd. Middlesbrough and London.

Sleights at war 1914-1918, The Hospital Years, compiled by Alan Whitwor